MANUAL *for* WOMEN

Danielle Bean

TAN·BOOKS

Gastonia, North Carolina

ISBN: 978-1-5051-1301-3

Printed and bound in India

TAN Books
Gastonia, North Carolina
www.TANBooks.com
2019

PRESENTED TO

_____

Name

_____

Date / Occasion

Personal Note

_____

_____

_____

_____

_____

_____

To the perfect example of feminine genius lived out with perfection, my mother and yours, the Blessed Virgin Mary. Thank you for praying me through my stumbling journey toward home.

*The woman's soul is fashioned as a shelter
in which other souls may unfold.*

ST. EDITH STEIN

CONTENTS

HOW TO USE THIS MANUAL

e at TAN Books are honored to present Catholic women with this next installment in our Manual Series, the *Manual for Women* by Danielle Bean. As with our other manuals—those for Spiritual Warfare, Eucharistic Adoration, Men, Conquering Deadly Sin, and Marian Devotion—this book is sure to become a treasured and much-leafed through volume for those who read it.

But that begs the question: how to read it? The first answer is, of course, anyway you want. And anywhere you want: at home, in the adoration chapel, at the YMCA or playground while the kids play, in the chapel of your convent, in bed, on the couch, at work (okay, maybe not at work unless you work for a Catholic publisher). But, regardless of where or when you read it, we would urge you to begin with Danielle's wonderful opening essay. She is many things: wife, mother, writer, editor, television personality, brand manager at CatholicMom.com, and more. But most fundamentally, at the very core of her being, Danielle is a devoted Catholic woman, one who knows the faith and lives it. She is conversant both with the Church's grand tradition and the best thinking and writing the Church offers her daughters today. She knows your triumphs, your failures, your joys, your sorrows. She is, in short, one of you.

As we don't want to keep you from the riches contained within any longer, let us close with the following advice which just might be the way you choose to delve into your *Manual for Women*. Enjoy!

Take this *Manual for Women* in one hand and a cup of coffee in the other . . . and get ready to pray, laugh, and receive the down-to-earth wisdom Danielle Bean has to offer in this book. Danielle has a delightful way of teaching us the beauty of the faith, while relating it to what's actually going on in our crazy-busy lives as women. You will find refreshment, hope, healing, and encouragement in the pages that follow!

JACKIE FRANCOIS ANGEL, SPEAKER, SONGWRITER, AND AUTHOR OF *FOREVER: A CATHOLIC DEVOTIONAL FOR YOUR MARRIAGE.*

May this manual help you, dear reader, on your path to heaven.

PART ONE

Being the Woman God Made You to Be

INTRODUCTION

Heaven better be real good," a struggling friend once complained to me over the phone as a stomach virus raged through her busy household. "Not just a bunch of people standing around talking to each other, but real good. Do you know what I mean?"

For sure I did.

Life is a messy thing. Sometimes, in the midst of pain and sacrifice, all we want is some tangible assurance that our efforts will be rewarded. As we struggle through piles of bills and car repairs, rebellious teenagers and cranky bosses, and all manner of foul weather and human weakness, we would just like a little dose of heavenly perfection now and then. Is that too much to ask?

There were no stomach viruses in the Garden of Eden. There were no rashes, no bug bites, no burnt toast, no anxiety, no depression, no exhaustion, no unpleasant work, and no sin. There were none of the evils and annoyances, big and small, that we post-fall humans find ourselves contending with every day.

Can you even imagine such a place? Most of us can't, because the world we are living in feels impossibly far away from paradise.

Do you ever think about original sin and get just a little bit annoyed at Eve? I mean, Eve had it made. There she was in her very own paradise, freshly created, beautiful, and intelligent. Her husband adored her, she knew no hunger or weakness, she had the perfect body, and she was surrounded by perfection and beauty in a natural world God had made just for her and her beloved man.

Why did she have to go and mess it all up?

In fairness to Eve, though, we must also ask why we continue to mess it all up. It is an inevitable part of the human experience to find out just how messed up the world is, sometimes in deeply personal and painful ways. We see it in war, broken families, addiction, violence, and abuse. But we see it in subtler ways too—sometimes in our own pride or jealousy, or our own temptation toward anger, lust, or greed.

What We Are Made For

And yet those of us who believe not only in original sin but also in the redemptive power of God want to know and do God's will in our lives. We want to fix the ways in which we and others are warped, wounded, and broken by sin. We want to be what God made us to be and calls us to be, despite our fallen nature. We want to take seriously the mission God calls us to.

But what might that be?

Ultimately, seeking to know who we are and what we are made for as women brings us back to the Garden of Eden. To know God's plan for human beings, and in particular God's plan for us as women, we must look to Eve, the first woman, and find out what we can learn from her story.

In the familiar story we read in the Old Testament book of Genesis, we first meet Eve, in all her perfection, when God creates her from one of Adam's ribs. When Adam sees Eve for the first time, he is overcome by her beauty and perfection.

"'This at last is bone of my bones and flesh of my flesh; she shall be called Woman, because she was taken out of Man.' Therefore a man leaves his father and his mother and cleaves to his wife, and they become one flesh" (Gn 2:23–24).

Adam's words of joy highlight the complementarity and connection between man and woman as God planned it and as it existed, in perfection, in our natural state. Woman is made for man; man is made for woman. The two become one. This beautiful description of the unity that God intends between the sexes is a popular reading at weddings. We like to be reminded that we were made good, we were made perfect, and we were made for one another. We like to remember God's original plan.

But let's read on. Because then sin creeps in—a less popular wedding reading, perhaps, but a real part of the story nonetheless. A serpent somehow enters the paradise Adam and Eve share, and he singles out Eve for temptation. We all know that God gave Adam and Eve all the fruit of the garden for eating except for the fruit of one tree, which he warned them not to eat from, lest they die.

Taking and Trusting

It is telling that the serpent does not tempt Eve by pointing out how delicious the fruit looks on the forbidden tree. Eve succumbs to a temptation that has little to do with the fruit itself. Instead, the serpent tempts her by suggesting that God is not to be trusted.

"The woman said to the serpent, 'We may eat of the fruit of the trees in the garden; but God said, "You shall not eat of the fruit of the tree which is in the midst of the garden, neither shall you touch it, lest you die."' But the serpent said to the woman, 'You will not die. For God knows that when you eat of it your eyes will be opened, and you will be like God, knowing good and evil'" (Gn 3:2–5).

You will not die.

The Father of Lies, in the form of a serpent, speaks the first of his lies to the first of humans. He paints a warped picture of a selfish God who is not to be trusted, a God who keeps good things only for himself.

Eve believes the lies. She believes, even if only for a moment, that God is not to be trusted. He will not provide good things. He is keeping good things from her, and so if she wants good things, she must take them for herself.

And have we not just described every sin? Every sin we might ever commit, or be tempted to commit, has little to do with the substance of the sin at the beginning. It begins with a lack of trust in God. We believe, even if only for a moment, Satan's lie that God is not to be trusted. He will not provide good things. He is keeping them from us, and so if we want good things, we must take them for ourselves.

Loss and Life-Giving Love

Sin always begins with taking instead of trusting.

But there are consequences for the taking. The ironic truth is that when we try to take good things instead of trusting in God's generous goodness, we lose good things altogether. When Adam and Eve disobey God and eat the forbidden fruit from the forbidden tree, their eyes are opened. They lose innocence and perfection; they find themselves naked and ashamed.

And then come the consequences, spelled out by God himself when he finds the sorry pair hiding in their shame. So many good things are forever lost because of their grasping. Men and women must now toil at work, suffer pain, death, and disunity, and battle against nature for their daily sustenance.

> To the woman he said, "I will greatly multiply your pain in childbearing; in pain you shall bring forth children, yet your desire shall be for your husband, and he shall rule over you." And to Adam he said, "Because you have listened to the voice of your wife, and have eaten of the tree of which I commanded you, 'You shall not eat of it,' cursed is the ground because of you; in toil you shall eat of it all the days of your life; thorns and thistles it shall bring forth to you; and you shall eat the plants of the field. In the sweat of your face you shall eat bread till you return to the ground, for out of it you were taken; you are dust, and to dust you shall return." (Gn 3:16–19)

A depressing litany of loss, pain, and suffering, is it not? And yet, there, in that moment, after God speaks these words of condemnation and punishment, Adam sees something that brings him hope. Something that promises new life. And it is such a sure hope that he dares give voice to it.

What did Adam see? He saw his wife. He saw Eve. He saw Woman.

In the very next line, we read, "The man called his wife's name Eve, because she was the mother of all living" (Gn 3:20).

The mother of all living. There, in that shared moment of sin, sorrow, shame, death, and loss, Adam saw the potential for life-giving love in the form of Woman. Eve would bring forth children, he dared to hope. She would be the mother of all living.

The mother of all living isn't just Eve. It's all women. It's me and it's you. It's your great grand-mother and your crabby Aunt Beatrice. It's the kind lady at your church who never married and has no children of her own. It's your mother, your sisters, your daughters, and your nieces.

Mother of all living is the ideal for which women were created. Adam's words describe the art of life-giving love that every woman is built for and uniquely created to bring forth in herself and others.

This is us. Even in the darkest of places, women bring life. We bring love. We bring hope to a fallen world.

Every Woman's Call

I can already hear some of you objecting.

"I cannot be mother of all living," you might be thinking, "I have never had a child, or I am not even married, or I am a religious sister, or my children are grown and gone, or I have lost my child, or I was never very good at motherhood anyway."

Of course, what we mean by "mother of all living" is not that every woman is destined to physically bear children of her own. What we mean is that every woman is uniquely made for the art of self-giving, life-giving, generous, nurturing love. These feminine strengths come from God and are manifested in each of us in unique ways, depending upon what God calls us to and the manner in which we respond to that call.

Perhaps instead of saying every woman is a mother (though I believe that is true), we might say every woman is called to mother. Mother is a verb. And it's what we do.

I have always found it interesting to note that the verb to father implies little involvement beyond the original act of impregnating a woman. But to mother implies a lifetime of love, work, and connection; we can even "mother" adults, friends, coworkers, and children who are not our own.

A woman who adopts a child and suffers through countless trials before, during, and after the adoption process to make that child feel accepted and loved is a mother. A woman who teaches students, noticing and caring for their smallest needs and rejoicing in their progress, is a mother. A woman who is moved by the suffering of others and donates her time, efforts, and resources to alleviate that suffering is a mother. The unmarried, childless nurse who talked me through labor with my first child, massaging my belly through contractions and speaking words of calm into my panic, is a mother.

Every woman mothers, and is called to mother, in different ways. This is not a culturally popular thing to say in today's world that denies differences between the sexes in the name of "equality" and "liberation." But we deny what is written on our hearts at our own peril. Our own peace, joy, and satisfaction in our life's work are at stake.

Success Redefined

In the name of "liberation," our culture might try to tell us that mothering, in all its forms, is somehow degrading and beneath us. We need to break free from the shackles of caregiving and claim our place in the boardroom.

And some women will choose the boardroom and find great success there. And thanks be to God for the women who do and who bring the gift of their feminine perspective to the working world. But far too often what we find out is that success and fulfillment as they are defined in the world look very different from the kind of success and fulfillment we naturally seek. The world feeds us a masculine ideal of "success." We women can achieve that and yet still feel a longing for something more meaningful in our lives.

"What is this?" I remember my college professor saying as he pointed to the engagement ring on my finger years ago. "You have great gifts, and you could really achieve something! What are you doing?"

I don't remember what I answered him, but I knew what I was doing. I was choosing marriage and family; I was responding to an undeniable calling that was written on my heart. I was rejecting a cultural idea of what my "success" should look like and instead trusting God to help my young husband and me to work out the details of paying the bills and achieving a worldly definition of "success," which I saw as a lesser good.

Not every woman's call will look like mine, but all human beings are built for relationship, and women are particularly gifted in the art of fostering connection and building bonds between human beings. We are all called to mother, and somehow, when we listen to what is etched upon our hearts, we know that "mothering," in all its forms, is the most meaningful and important work we can ever do.

Women, more so than men, have an instinctive knowledge and understanding of the value of human connection. It's why so many women leave high-paying jobs, if they can afford to, or even if they can barely afford to, in order to care for their children. It's why women, more so than men, gravitate toward "caregiving" roles in their families, as at-home moms and as caregivers to their aging parents. It's why even women in the workplace are most likely to be the ones who note and act upon the feelings and needs of others, looking to connect, build relationships, and make others feel known and loved, even in the secular, professional world.

And our world needs our motherhood. It needs yours, and it needs mine. As the great St. Edith Stein, converted Jew, philosopher, Carmelite nun, and martyr who died at Auschwitz, once wrote, "Everywhere the need exists for maternal sympathy and help, and thus we are able to recapitulate in the one word motherliness that which we have developed as the characteristic value of woman. Only, the motherliness must be that which does not remain within the narrow circle of blood relations or of personal friends; but in accordance with the model of the Mother of Mercy, it must have its root in universal divine love for all who are there, belabored and burdened."[1]

Mary as Our Model

As St. Edith Stein points out, when it comes to womanhood, Mary is our model. We have already looked to Eve in order to understand God's original plan for women, but we have also noted the ways in which Eve messed up that plan, by rejecting the will of God, and the ways in which we continue to do the same. To more fully understand

---

[1] *The Collected Works of Edith Stein*, eds. L. Gelber and Romaeus Leuven, trans. Freda Mary Oben, vol. 2, *Essays on Woman* (Washington: ICS Publications, 2017) 258.

God's plan for women, we should look to the example of someone who did not mess up at all: Mary, the mother of Jesus.

As Edith Stein further notes, "As woman was the first to be tempted, so did God's message of grace come first to a woman, and each time woman's assent determined the destiny of humanity as a whole."[2]

Eve said no, but Mary said yes.

Let's take a look at some of the ways Mary demonstrates for us both the perfect response to God's call and the perfect example of womanhood, for it is in imitating Mary that we may best understand, embrace, cultivate, and share our uniquely feminine gifts and strengths, among which may be included receptivity, sensitivity, compassion, beauty, and generosity.

---

2 Ibid., 65.

I

FEMININE GIFT OF RECEPTIVITY

Many years ago, when I was a young, unmarried woman, I remember talking with a group of friends about the concept of pregnancy. To me, the idea of the human body being capable of receiving, nurturing, and ultimately giving birth to another human person was astonishing and beautiful. The fact the female body—my body even—was capable of such a feat was the most fascinating and incredible fact of nature I could imagine. One of my young, male friends, however, disagreed.

"That sounds horrifying," he said. "Like growing an alien inside your body."

Neither of us knew what we were talking about, of course, but I recalled that conversation years later when I was pregnant for the first time. Not every moment was magical; I experienced incessant nausea and exhaustion in the first trimester (a little nod to Eve in the Garden of Eden). But I did note that my response to my pregnancy was more naturally one of joy and wonder at the process than that of my anxious husband.

For sure, I had my "alien" moments (natural childbirth, anyone?), but I felt connected to my unborn baby in a way that my husband could not fully understand. As nature intends, the fact that my daughter developed and grew inside of me facilitated a bond between us that felt as natural as breathing.

Our bodies matter. Our bodies are a physical expression of who we are and who we are called to be. The fact that female and male bodies differ in fundamental ways is a meaningful expression of our different gifts and vocations as male and female.

"The body and only the body," wrote St. John Paul II in his teachings on Theology of the Body, "is capable of making visible what is invisible, the spiritual and the divine."[3]

Female bodies, whether they ever realize the potential for it or not, are designed by God to be receptive to new life. We have wombs that can welcome a newly-conceived human being and provide the perfect, protected space in which that person can develop and grow. When a woman becomes pregnant, even before she takes a test and knows about the new life she carries within, her body knows and begins diverting resources—blood, oxygen, and nutrition—toward that tiny person. Our bodies are open to life.

---

3   Pope John Paul II, General Audiences, Theology of the Body, February 20, 1980, 19:4.

Mary Said Yes

The receptivity of our bodies to other human beings reflects an even more beautiful spiritual truth about the nature of women. We are receptive. We are open to others. We are uniquely designed by God to be a place of welcome and nurturing for others. Can there be any more beautiful gift than that?

For the perfect example of feminine receptivity to others and to the will of God, we need look no further than Mary at the Annunciation.

When the angel visited Mary and told her "you will conceive in your womb and bear a son, and you shall call his name Jesus" (Lk 1:31), she was confused about how this could possibly happen. And so the angel explained. "And the angel said to her, 'The Holy Spirit will come upon you, and the power of the Most High will overshadow you; therefore the child to be born will be called holy, the Son of God" (Lk 1:35).

I don't know about you, but I would still find this pretty difficult to understand. I am sure Mary did too, but she most definitely understood that what the angel proposed was the will of God, and she responded accordingly. "And Mary said, 'Behold, I am the handmaid of the Lord; let it be done to me according to your word'" (Lk 1:35, 38).

Mary said yes. Without fully understanding what was happening and how it would happen, and knowing that it might cost her dearly, Mary said yes. As a consequence of Mary's receptivity to the will of God, Jesus entered her womb, Jesus entered the world, and all of humanity could be saved from sin. Eve's no was redeemed by Mary's yes.

Think of the beautiful parallel between Mary's pregnancy with Jesus and the gift of self that Jesus provides us in the Eucharist. In the Eucharist, out of immeasurable love for each of us, Jesus says, "This is my body, given up for you." At the Annunciation, out of immeasurable love for God, Mary says, "Let it be done to me, according to your word."

As women, we have the unique privilege of engaging in actions, physically and spiritually, that closely correspond with Jesus's and Mary's examples of self-giving love. Many of the messages aimed at women in the modern world, however, stand in stark contrast to Mary's yes. Receptivity to others is seen as weakness. Our bodies' ability to become pregnant is a liability. In the medical profession, female fertility is treated as a disease. "My body, given up for you" and "Let it be done to me to me according to your word" are foolish, sexist notions. Instead, "my body, my choice" is a popular mantra in the name of female liberation.

And yet I cannot think of anything more sexist than to tell women that there is something wrong with them because their bodies and souls are different from men's. There is nothing more sexist than to take masculine definitions of "success" and "fulfillment" and demand that women measure up to them instead of the kinds of success and fulfillment we are naturally inclined toward as women. True sexism is telling women that they must squash, kill, and hide their unique capacity for receiving and nurturing new life, both physically and spiritually, in order to be truly happy.

As women, we have the opportunity to imitate Mary's example through our receptivity to new life, quite literally, through pregnancy, but also spiritually, through our openness to God and others in our everyday lives. The people God places in our lives are living, breathing manifestations of his will for us. The people God entrusts to our care are the ones we are called to say yes to and to be open to receiving. They might be your own husband and children, grandchildren, nieces, and nephews, neighborhood kids, the elderly, the poor, your coworkers, your sick mother-in-law, friends at your parish, or that lonely teenager who lives down the street.

All human beings are worthy of love, and the ones God places in your life are both a gift and a calling. A calling to motherhood, and a gift that our world desperately needs. Do you have people in your life who need love and caring? We all do. It might be your family members, your neighbors, your coworkers, or the poor in your community. The people God places in our lives are a manifestation of God's will for us. They are our call to a vocation of love. As St. John Paul II once described:

At Christmas time the Church puts before the eyes of our spirit the Motherhood of Mary, and it does so on the first day of the new year. It does so, also, to highlight the dignity of every mother, to define and recall the significance of motherhood, not only in the life of every man, but also in the whole of human culture. Motherhood is woman's vocation. It is an eternal vocation, and it is also a contemporary vocation.

"The Mother who understands everything and embraces each of us with her heart": these are words of a song, sung by young people in Poland, which come into my mind at this moment. The song goes on to announce that today the world is particularly "hungry and thirsty" for that motherhood, which is woman's vocation "physically" and "spiritually", as it is Mary's.[4]

---

4 Pope St. John Paul II, General Audience, January 10, 1979.

2

FEMININE GIFT OF SENSITIVITY

hen the lights came on after the movie ended, my family turned to me and laughed.

"What?" I asked, eyes puffy and nose red from sobbing.

I learned long ago that I am a crier. I accept it. There comes a point in pretty much any movie where there is a particularly poignant scene, a gesture of love, or a moment of beauty and joy, and the tears just start flowing. It's OK. That's what Kleenex is for.

I used to be embarrassed by my ability to spill tears at a moment's notice, while watching movies or Subaru commercials, while reading novels or my son's book report, while witnessing a tender moment between my children or words of encouragement from a father to his son. But I have come to accept my tears as an outward sign of a feminine gift of sensitivity, one that every woman has, that is expressed in each of us differently.

One Christmas, as my extended family gathered to exchange gifts, my brother's wife opened a small gift from him. It was a tiny box with the label of her favorite, expensive perfume. She opened the box and found it was . . . empty. The sales clerk had neglected to check if the bottle was actually in the box before selling it to my brother, and so he had lovingly bought and wrapped an empty box as a Christmas gift for his wife.

It was funny. My entire family laughed out loud. And then I burst into tears.

Not for the disappointment of the gift—for sure my sister-in-law would get her perfume—but for the feelings involved. My brother had been so thoughtful in noting his wife's favorite perfume, and so generous in buying it, despite their tight budget as newlyweds and its high price tag. He had been so careful to wrap that tiny box in shiny paper and tie it up with a beautiful bow as a gesture of love for his bride.

I was fully aware of all the beautiful feelings behind the disappointing gift, and they moved me to tears.

Not all women are criers, of course, but we are all feel-ers. We are all gifted with a unique feminine capacity to be sensitive to the needs and feelings of others. We readily see and understand others in a way that most men do not.

Mary Sees Others Too

Mary exemplifies the feminine gift of sensitivity in a particular way in the familiar story of the wedding at Cana. She and Jesus attend a wedding where the newlywed couple find themselves in the embarrassing situation of having run out of wine. "On the third day there was a marriage at Cana in Galilee, and the mother of Jesus was there; Jesus was also invited to the marriage, with his disciples. When the wine failed, the mother of Jesus said to him, 'They have no wine'" (Jn 2:1–3).

Running out of wine was awkward, but in the grand scheme of things, not a very big deal. The couple might be embarrassed on their special day, but in the end, no one would truly be hurt and folks would move on with their lives. No real harm done.

But Mary, in her sensitivity to the needs and feelings of others, noticed the young couple's moment of need and wanted to help. Her example demonstrates the importance of caring about the "small stuff" of others' needs and feelings. It is worth noting, too, that though Mary was the one who noticed and called attention to the couple's need, she was not ultimately the one who could help them. But she knew who could.

Despite Jesus's protests that his hour 'has not yet come," Mary persists, as only a woman can, in her confidence that he can and will help. "His mother said to the servants, 'Do whatever he tells you'" (Jn 2:5).

And so it was that Jesus, at the nudging of his mother, performed his first public miracle of changing water into wine. Jesus's responsiveness to his mother's wishes, despite the fact that his hour "has not yet come" and despite the fact that running out of wine is not the end of the world, conveys a deep respect for the feminine role she was playing out in that moment.

In fact, when Jesus protests Mary's suggestion, he calls her "woman." "And Jesus said to her, 'O woman, what have you to do with me? My hour has not yet come'" (Jn 2:4).

Jesus's use of the word woman here, in reference to his mother, highlights the uniquely feminine role he sees her playing. She, for her part and in a special way at that moment in the lives of herself and her Son, fully embodies the feminine gift of sensitivity to the needs and feelings of others.

As women today, we have the opportunity to imitate Mary's perfect example of womanhood by embracing our own feminine sensitivity. You don't have to cry at movies to do this. Many women practice sensitivity in caring for their families. We might notice when our husband seems stressed and make plans for a quiet evening. We might notice when a toddler seems "off" and check him for illness. We might notice when a teen is withdrawn and make efforts to find out what he is struggling with.

But the gift of feminine sensitivity is not only practiced inside of families. Women in the workplace might notice a coworker's financial struggles and look for a way to help. Women might notice a need for adult day care, food for the hungry, shelter for the homeless, or childcare for single moms in their communities and look for a way to fill these needs.

Like Mary, we may not always be the one who will ultimately meet the needs of others, but we can use our unique capacity for noticing the details of others' lives, for understanding how they feel, and for calling attention to their needs in order to help get them met. We can look for God's will in the needs of the people he places in our care and in our lives. Truly, we can "mother" those around us with sensitivity and be that embodiment of human love and connection for them. Women alone can, in imitation of Mary, be what St. John Paul II called "the Mother who understands everything and embraces each of us with her heart."[5]

---

5   Pope St. John Paul II, General Audience, January 10, 1979.

3

FEMININE GIFT OF COMPASSION

always laugh when I see splashy headlines on trashy women's magazines at the supermarket checkout: "Are you and your man compatible?"

Compatible. Funny word. It's a derivative of the Latin word *compati*, meaning to "suffer with." What Cosmopolitan and others like it are really asking is, "Are you and your man ready to suffer together?" This question is actually an important one for couples to consider, one that popular magazines probably would not ask in a million years. The idea of "suffering together" truly is a more authentic understanding of the meaning of marriage from a Catholic perspective, but that's for later in this book.

Yes, the word compassion does have the same roots as compatible. It means to "suffer with," and compassion is another gift that women are uniquely capable of practicing with others.

Years ago, I had a job working as a program director in a nursing home. I had the task of coming up with appropriate activity and entertainment options for each of the residents, according to their interests and abilities. With the more able-bodied residents, activities were easy to plan. We met for morning exercise classes, went on scenic train rides, discussed characters and plots in book clubs, and enjoyed lunch at local restaurants.

But Elsa was a different story. Elsa was seriously incapacitated after having suffered multiple strokes. She spent her days in bed, awake, but mostly unresponsive to others. How was I to come up with an activity plan for Elsa?

I need not have worried. Shirley, a volunteer and friend of Elsa's who came into the nursing home multiple times per week, had that all figured out.

"Elsa just wants someone to be there," she explained.

Shirley would spend entire afternoons with Elsa, brushing her hair, painting her nails, and updating her on goings-on with family and friends. But mostly Shirley would just sit with Elsa, holding her hand or patting her arm, simply being present to her friend. Whatever things Elsa suffered in those days—physically or emotionally, in ways we could see or could not see—she did not suffer them alone. Shirley was present in her suffering. She was there with her, blessing her friend with the gift of feminine compassion.

Once, at a meeting of my parish women's group, we broke into small groups for discussion topics. One of the discussion questions was "What opportunities do you have to love and serve others every day?"

Some women at my table went first, describing how they care for small children or elderly parents, or how they smile at people in the post office when they seem to be having a bad day. These were all good examples, but I was particularly struck by what Ruth shared. Ruth was an older woman who had never married or had children of her own. She shared some of the ways that she had cared for family members or others' children throughout her life, but the main way Ruth felt she had served others was through her work as a nurse, especially during World War II. She told us stories of tending to the wounds of soldiers when others were afraid to be near them because everyone knew they were going to die.

"I got so it didn't bother me," she said, "I didn't do much for them, but I was with them. They just needed someone to be with them."

Even though she is retired from nursing now, Ruth still takes calls from the hospital when a patient is in danger of dying alone.

"They call me, and if I can, I'll go and sit with them," she said. "If I don't, who will? They just don't want to be alone."

It is beautiful to think of the number of patients Ruth has "mothered" over the years with her gift of feminine compassion simply being present to others in their suffering.

Mary's Model of Compassionate Love

To be the mother of Jesus was a privilege and a joy, but from the very beginning, Mary's motherhood was tinged with a hint of the suffering to come. When Jesus was a baby, and Mary and Joseph brought him to present him at the temple, the prophet Simeon spoke the truth to them: "Simeon blessed them and said to Mary his mother, 'Behold, this child is set for the fall and rising of many in Israel, and for a sign that is spoken against (and a sword will pierce through your own soul also), that thoughts out of many hearts may be revealed" (Lk 2:34–35).

A sword will pierce your soul. Imagine Mary's thoughts upon hearing those words. What kind of piercing would it be?

And of course, we know now that the sword that pierced Mary's heart and soul was the passion and death of her son, Jesus. Mary was present with Jesus through every stage of his beating, whipping, torture, bleeding, cross-carrying, and crucifixion. She sat at the foot of the cross, helpless as he suffered, nailed to the cross above her; she received his lifeless body and wept for loss of her child, who was also her Lord.

Just as God pronounced to Eve in the Garden of Eden all those years ago, motherhood comes with its own unique forms of suffering. Many of us know the kind of suffering we risk when we pour out our very selves for the love of others, whether they be our children, our husband, our siblings, our parents, or our friends, but few of us have suffered the pain of watching helplessly as our innocent child is tortured and crucified before our eyes. But Mary knows that kind of pain. She willingly endured it for love of Jesus, to be present to him in his suffering. She could do nothing to relieve his physical suffering, but she could be a source of motherly, feminine compassion to him as he lived out his passion and death.

Jesus knew the worth of this gift of Mary's motherly compassion, and he acknowledged it, even as he hung on the cross, bleeding and dying for love of you and me. In his last moments, as he suffered terrible physical pain, he saw us and he loved us. He asked God the Father to forgive his tormentors; he forgave the "good thief" who hung beside him on a cross of his own, and he gave us his mother. At the foot of the cross, he saw the gift of Mary's compassionate motherhood, and he chose to give that gift to all mankind. "When Jesus saw his mother, and the disciple whom he loved standing near, he said to his mother, 'Woman, behold your son!' Then he said to the disciple, 'Behold, your mother!' And from that hour the disciple took her to his own home" (Jn 19:26–27).

With this generous gesture, Jesus highlights the gift of Mary's compassion and multiplies her motherhood so that she might become the mother to all and the truest example of motherly love for every one of us.

Sometimes the worst part of suffering is feeling alone in it. As the perfect model of womanhood, Mary knew that, and she offered the gift of compassion as a silent witness to Jesus's passion and death. She simply was present to him in his time of suffering, and she is with us in ours.

As St. Jerome, Father and Doctor of the Church, observes about Mary's motherhood of not only Jesus but her spiritual motherhood of us all, "Even while living in the world, the heart of Mary was so filled with motherly tenderness and compassion for men that no one ever suffered so much for their own pains, as Mary suffered for the pains of her children."

Let us aim to be mothers like that, true sources of womanly compassion, true companions, and ever-present sources of silent consolation, to all those whom God brings into our lives.

4

FEMININE GIFT OF BEAUTY

o you think of yourself as beautiful? Beautiful is a complicated word for many women. Most of us are not comfortable thinking of ourselves as beautiful. Images of Vogue magazine covers might come to mind, and we begin to calculate all the ways we don't measure up. We're lacking high cheekbones, lustrous hair, unwrinkled skin, long legs, or a flat stomach.

But let's think about real feminine beauty for a minute. Can you think of someone you know who might fit the world's standards for physical attractiveness but has negative personality traits that make her unattractive in the end? And further, can you think of someone you know who might not meet traditional standards for physical beauty but whose eyes shine with radiant joy and whose face lights up with what can be called nothing less than "beauty" when she smiles? I think most of us can think of examples that fit both descriptions.

Consider St. Teresa of Calcutta. Standing all of five feet tall, the tiny, wrinkled nun was unlikely to grace the cover of Vogue during her lifetime, and yet she had an undeniable, radiant beauty that was clear to anyone in her presence. Hers was a uniquely feminine beauty that came from her full embrace of her motherly vocation and the sense of purpose and fulfillment she found in loving God and serving the poor.

We might vary in our levels of attractiveness, but all women do share a natural feminine beauty in our bodies and in our souls. Throughout all of history, the works of great artists celebrated female beauty, and even our modern culture recognizes the power of feminine beauty, though it does not get it quite right. Modern corporations use the power of feminine beauty to sell everything from fast food to motor oil, and one particularly vile "industry" exploits our beauty by divorcing it from our humanity in the form of pornography.

Real feminine beauty, however, has little to do with what the "world"—in the Catholic sense of "the world, the flesh, and the devil"—focuses on. In his Catechesis on Human Love, St. John Paul II writes, "The whole exterior of the woman's body, its particular look, the qualities that stand with the power of perennial attraction . . . are in strict accordance with motherhood."[6]

What he means by this is that women are most authentically and truly women when we embrace

---

6　Pope St. John Paul II, General Audiences, Theology of the Body, March 12, 1980, 21:5.

our natural gift of nurturing, self-giving love. Our bodies are a physical expression of that vocation. We are most authentically beautiful when we are most authentically ourselves—the powerful, beautiful women God made us to be.

Eye for Beauty

Because we tend to notice and pay attention to the smallest of details, women also have a gift for finding beauty, highlighting it, and bringing it into the world in a way that enhances the human experience. Even women who are not particularly gifted "homemakers," like those who iron sheets and set the table with fresh flowers, find ways to bring beauty, order, peace, and comfort into our homes and places of work. We might give a bookcase a fresh coat of paint, organize a desk drawer, put a colorful ribbon in a little girl's hair. None of these gestures may be necessary, but they are the kind of things that add a bit of beauty and pleasure to our daily experiences. Small things add joy and meaning to our lives in a way that is hard to quantify.

More important than homemaking, though, women readily see the beauty of human connection and relationship, and we value these in a way that protects and nourishes them, to the benefit of all.

"Enjoy the little things in life," a poster that hangs in my office reads, "Because one day you will look back and realize they were the big things."

It's true, isn't it? When we look back over our lives, it's not the big things that we cherish and miss. It's the ordinary gift of everyday routines. We look back at old pictures, and we don't remember what was in our bank accounts or what was in the news that day. We love, and we cherish the memory of a small baby's smile or a toddler's messy face. We remember an old plaque that hung on the wall in our childhood home and attach great meaning to it. We remember the smell of our grandmother's perfume, or the touch of our father's hand. We recall the wallpaper in our bedroom and the hours we spent there, reading books or playing card games with siblings. It's the small stuff that gives joy and meaning to our lives.

Mary as Model of Beauty

Once again, we find a perfect model in Mary. She manifests for us the ideal of the feminine value of and appreciation for beauty through her actions (and inactions) as we read about them in the Gospel of Luke. Do you remember the scene when Jesus was born? "And suddenly there was with the angel a multitude of the heavenly host praising God and saying, 'Glory to God in the highest, and on earth peace among men with whom he is pleased!' When the angels went away from them into heaven, the shepherds said to one another, 'Let us go over to Bethlehem and see this thing that has happened, which the Lord has made known to us.' And they went with haste, and found Mary and Joseph, and the babe lying in a manger" (Lk 2:13–16).

It is a familiar story to us all, but try to imagine for a moment the drama of this scene as it occurred in real life. Jesus's birth was the greatest event in the history of man. There were singing angels in the sky and shepherds arriving to worship, and Jesus, God made man, in the form of a tiny infant, sleeps, lying in a manger.

So what did Mary do in this momentous, historic moment? What did she do? What did she say? She did nothing, and she said nothing; she quietly and lovingly observed all that was happening around her. "But Mary kept all these things, pondering them in her heart" (Lk 2:19).

She kept all these things and pondered them in her heart. In this great and historic moment, Mary simply soaked up the beauty and the meaning of it all. She quietly observed the Incarnation; she quietly welcomed shepherds who came to worship her infant son Jesus; she quietly kept these things, held them close to her heart, and pondered their deeper meaning, basking in the beauty of it all.

Here, Mary offers a perfect example of the feminine value of appreciating the significant, even though small, things that build bonds and connect us as people. It is women who recognize and nurture the small but important things in human relationships. We remember to send a birthday card.

We recall Grandpa's favorite dessert and make it for him when he visits. We thank our child's baseball coach for the extra attention he gave during practice. We notice our sister's new hair color and compliment her on it.

These are the small things that give true meaning and add beauty to human connections and relationships. Our feminine instincts tell us that meaning and worth are not necessarily found in showy displays or lots of words. Our instincts nudge us to nurture the true beauty that can only be found in real connection with others and is fostered by those "small things" we ponder in our hearts.

Pondering in Her Heart

Later, when Jesus is a young boy and he is lost and then found three days later in the temple, Mary is confused by his words and actions. "After three days they found him in the temple, sitting among the teachers, listening to them and asking them questions; and all who heard him were amazed at his understanding and answers. And when they saw him they were astonished; and his mother said to him, 'Son, why have you treated us so? Behold, your father and I have been looking for you anxiously'" (Lk 2:46–48).

If Mary was astonished to find Jesus teaching in the temple, she must have been even more astonished by his answer to her question. "And he said to them, 'How is it that you sought me? Did you not know that I must be in my Father's house?' And they did not understand the saying which he spoke to them" (Lk 2:49–50).

And yet, once again, we find that Mary, in her consternation, does not grow impatient and demand answers. Instead, she quietly observes and ponders. "And he went down with them and came to Nazareth, and was obedient to them; and his mother kept all these things in her heart" (Lk 2:51).

We don't know how much Mary knew about how Jesus was to save the world from sin or when she knew it, but we see her here, pondering the beauty of God's plan. Respectfully, she watches it unfold in the life of her little family.

We can do the same. Mysteries of wonder and beauty unfold before our eyes, in the ordinary goings-on of our lives, every day. What a gift and an opportunity we have as women in our homes, communities, and workplaces! We can be attentive to the beauty of everyday human relationships and connections and invite others to see it too.

5

FEMININE GIFT OF GENEROSITY

remember once, years ago, I struggled to make a Mother's Day card for my mom. I was about seven years old at the time, and I had written "THANK YOU for . . ." on the front of the card. I was going to list a few of the things my mother did for my family and me on the inside, but there was only room for three or four, and I found it impossible to narrow down the list.

What were the most important things, I wondered. Driving all of us all over town for sports and sleepovers? Cleaning the bathroom? Doing the laundry? Reading us stories? Making breakfasts and lunches and dinners? Cleaning the dishes? Buying us new clothes while she wore old ones? I was in awe of my mother's seemingly tireless generosity in service to our family, and even at a young age, I knew no card could adequately express gratitude for the blessing that she was. And she still is that kind of blessing to her grown children and grandchildren today.

Perhaps you were blessed with a good mom like I was, but even if you weren't, I'll bet there are women

in your life who have astonished you with their
maternal generosity. It might have been a teacher
who was steadfast and patient with you through
a tough time. It might have been an aunt, grand-
mother, or neighbor who took care of you when
you were small. It might have been a girlfriend who
dropped everything to come and be with you at a
time when you really needed her.

When we think of generous women, sometimes
only the famous ones come to mind—"rock stars"
like St. Mother Teresa, St. Zelie Martin, or St. Elizabeth of Hungary who cared for the poor, fed the
hungry, and raised children who became saints
themselves. But even ordinary women are capable
of extraordinary generosity. St. John Paul II knows
this: "Necessary emphasis should be placed on the
'genius of women', not only by considering great
and famous women of the past or present, but
also those ordinary women who reveal the gift of
their womanhood by placing themselves at the service of others in their everyday lives. For in giving
themselves to others each day women fulfil their
deepest vocation. Perhaps more than men, women
acknowledge the person, because they see persons
with their hearts."[7]

---

7   Pope St. John Paul II, Letter of Pope John Paul II to Women,
    1995.

Feminine Genius

Here in this passage, St. John Paul II praises women for the gift they make of themselves in service to others, every day. That means you and me, and every "ordinary" woman you know. We are all gifted with an extraordinary capacity for self-giving love.

This part of the "genius of women" is manifested in our bodies. Even women who never conceive a child or give birth have, on average, 5–10 percent more body fat than men. We have hips and wombs and breasts. From gestation to lactation, our bodies are designed to receive and nurture new life from our very physical selves. Our bodies, feeding upon our own biological and nutritional resources, provide the perfect place for an unborn child to grow.

Once again, a physical reality mirrors a spiritual one: we give from ourselves for the good of others. And it is in giving of ourselves to others that we find our real identity and real satisfaction.

Mary Models Generosity

We've already looked at Mary's generosity in terms of her receptivity to God's will at the Annunciation. Immediately following the Annunciation, however, she exemplifies a new and different kind of generosity. Remember how the angel told Mary that her cousin Elizabeth was expecting a child? "And behold, your kinswoman Elizabeth in her old age has conceived a son; and this is the sixth month for her who was called barren" (Lk 1:36).

The angel did not explicitly tell Mary that her cousin was in need, or even suggest that she should go to her, but that is exactly what Mary did. "In those days Mary arose and went with haste into the hill country, to a city of Judah, and she entered the house of Zechariah and greeted Elizabeth. And when Elizabeth heard the greeting of Mary, the babe leaped in her womb; and Elizabeth was filled with the Holy Spirit and she exclaimed with a loud cry, 'Blessed are you among women, and blessed is the fruit of your womb!'" (Lk 1:39–42).

I like that the Gospel tells us that Mary went "with haste." It would have been perfectly understandable if Mary had taken a few days to absorb what the angel had told her. Becoming the mother of the Messiah was no small thing. And yet, upon hearing of her cousin's pregnancy, Mary did not focus on herself. She arose and went "with haste" to be of service to her cousin.

Mary's fast-acting example demonstrates the importance of service to others. And what happiness and consolation she brought to Elizabeth! Her unborn baby leapt for joy within her womb and she was filled with the Holy Spirit.

Mary, too, was filled with the Holy Spirit. The public praise she gives to God in her cousin's presence is an outward gesture of giving and generosity to all. "My soul magnifies the Lord, and my spirit rejoices in God, my savior" (Lk 1:46–47).

Mary's "magnificat" that follows is a beautiful song of praise and thanksgiving for the goodness of God. It is a generous outpouring of her very soul, out of love of God and gratitude for his many blessings.

> And Mary said, "My soul magnifies the Lord,
> and my spirit rejoices in God my Savior,
> for he has regarded the low estate of his
>   handmaiden.
> For behold, henceforth all generations will call
>   me blessed;
> for he who is mighty has done great things for
>   me,
> and holy is his name.
> And his mercy is on those who fear him
> from generation to generation.
> He has shown strength with his arm,
> he has scattered the proud in the imagination
>   of their hearts,
> he has put down the mighty from their thrones,
> and exalted those of low degree;
> he has filled the hungry with good things,
> and the rich he has sent empty away.
> He has helped his servant Israel,
> in remembrance of his mercy,
> as he spoke to our fathers,

to Abraham and to his posterity for ever." (Lk
1:46–55)

This public display is different from the quiet
"keeping and pondering" she will do later, after
Jesus's birth. Her perfect example of both vocal
rejoicing and quiet pondering teach us that there
is room in the perfection of the feminine soul for
both. There is a time for going out of ourselves in
service to others, a time for speaking out loudly and
sharing the goodness of God, and a time for quiet
focus on more hidden, but still important, things.

The most generous aspect of Mary's visit in this
story is that she brought Christ to her cousin Elizabeth. Quite literally, she brought Jesus, hidden in
her womb, to her cousin and her cousin's unborn
baby. But her beautiful words of praise bring an
awareness of great joy to all who hear them.

We practice a particularly feminine kind of generosity when we meet others in their time of need,
as Mary did for Elizabeth, and bring them Christ
through our actions and our words. We may not
carry Christ in our womb, but we can carry him in
our hearts. May our actions and our words speak
the truth of God's greatness and love to others: "For
he who is mighty has done great things for me, and
holy is his name" (Lk 1:49).

6

GETTING PRACTICAL

or me, one of the most frustrating parts about considering the beautiful ideas of God's plan for women, by looking to the first woman, Eve, the perfect woman Mary, and the writings of the saints, is that they're just that: ideas.

As inspiring as it is to consider the beautiful ways in which God created women with gifts and strengths and a unique capacity to bless the world with the feminine practice of self-giving, life-giving love, what does that have to do with my today, where I am fighting off a cold, I've been on hold with the gas company for forty-five minutes, and there is a pile of greasy dishes in the sink?

Where do all the beautiful ideas and ideals go when the rubber meets the road? It is there in the disconnect between the beautiful ideal and our real world, which so often falls so short of that ideal, that many of us find discouragement and disillusionment.

And so we have our work cut out for us. Here in this section we will begin to consider some of the aspects of life women struggle with most, along with some practical ideas for ways to turn ideas into action, in light of what we know to be true.

Personal Prayer

Do you have time set aside every day to pray? Even just five minutes in the morning before the kids get up or your work day starts?

Now I know what some of you are thinking: I hope she's not going to start lecturing me about prayer time, because I am busy!

And I get it. We are busy. Whether you are a mother at home with small children, a working mom with teens, a single woman with a demanding job, or a retiree caring for your grandkids three days a week, we all have a lot on our plates. And it's been my experience that our duties and obligations often multiply to fill the space we allot to them. The result is a lot of busy women walking around feeling distracted and frazzled, worried that they are not focused on the right things but unsure how to fix it, because there is just so much to do.

We will get to time management a little later, but for now this is what I have to say to you: you do have five minutes. It may not be at precisely the same time every day in a pristine and silent house, but you do have five minutes, every day, to devote to connecting with God. It's just a matter of choosing to spend those five minutes in prayer.

And the good news is that once you find your five minutes and dedicate yourself to spending that time in prayer, the five minutes grow, and you discover that you have even more time that you can spend—and want to spend—in conversation with God.

Prayer is a discipline, but we are built for it. Human beings are made for communion. We naturally create bonds with other human beings in our lives in the form of friends and family, but these connections are all imperfect, lesser versions of the greatest communion we are meant to have with God. Whether we know it or not, communion with God is our ultimate purpose as human beings. We cannot know true and perfect communion with God until the next life, but that longing and aching we sometimes feel, that gnawing notion that there "must be something more," is our built-in longing for God.

We might try to fill that emptiness we sometimes feel with other things—food, sex, money, or human relationships—and it might feel good for a little while, but in the end, everything that is not God will disappoint us.

We need a relationship with God in order to be happy, and we cannot have a relationship with someone we never take time to talk to.

So now that we have established that you need daily time for prayer, you might be wondering what that might look like? Is it daily Mass? Is it an hour a day on your knees in the adoration chapel? Is it five minutes of listening to inspiring music and opening your heart to God on the drive into work? Is it praying a Rosary while walking on your lunch break? Is it half an hour of reading the daily readings and reflecting on their meaning for your life?

It's all of these things, but then again it might be none of these things. Only you can determine what your daily prayer routine should look like, taking into consideration your life circumstances, your duties and obligations, and your own preferences. There is not a one-size-fits-all prescription for personal prayer.

As Natural as Breathing

Once you have established the habit of daily prayer, you might be surprised by how much you enjoy it. You really are built for communion with God after all, and the more you do it, the more natural and wonderful it will feel to connect with God on a regular basis.

Daily prayer can begin to open up your heart to possibilities of ways you can connect with God throughout your day, even in moments when you are very busy.

When it comes to daily prayer, I like to think of the sweetness of the close relationship I enjoyed with each of my children when they were very small. Each of my children, around the time they were beginning to crawl and walk, had a stage where they were intensely exploring the world, but also intensely focused on me. They would play and experiment with objects, toys, and other people, but they also would continually turn back to me, come back to me, and reconnect. I was their "home base."

In every event, no matter how small, they turned to me to share it. If they fell and bumped their head, they turned to me for comfort. If they stacked a pile of blocks to create a tall tower and were pleased with their accomplishment, they turned to me with a beaming smile.

This is a normal part of healthy child development, where a consistent, loving caregiver gives a child the security he or she needs to discover the world and expand horizons a little bit at a time. Returning to "home base" assures them that they are safe and well-cared-for, and fortifies them for the adventures that lie ahead.

I like to think I still play that role for my children, even though they are much older now and some of them are living on their own. I always want to be a source of security for them, a sure connection that allows them to take risks and grow. I call my own mother regularly for just that sort of "check-in" myself.

When it comes to our relationship with God, it can be helpful to reflect on human parent-child relationships because God tells us that he is our loving Father and we are his precious children.

Just as my toddlers once did with me, we can turn to God in all the things, big things and small things, happy things and sad things, that happen to us throughout our busy days. Before we begin any task, we can pause for a moment and offer our work to God. When we suffer some pain or disappointment, we can turn to God in our hearts and offer our sufferings to him. When we face a difficult challenge, we can turn our thoughts to God, asking for courage and strength.

In this way, our time set aside for prayer, where we truly connect with and nurture our relationship with him, can be extended throughout the rest of our day.

Don't expect perfection from yourself, though, especially as you are beginning a new practice of prayer. There come times for all of us when we pray for strength, but then we choose weakness instead. In times like these, instead of giving way to the temptation to despair, we must pick ourselves up, reconnect with God, and keep moving forward.

Even great saints struggled through prayer sometimes, but it is always in that constant, real connection with God that we find true meaning and purpose in our lives. Even when we fail to pray, still we are created for union with God.

In my own discouraged moments, when I feel that my prayer life falls far short of the ideal, I like to reflect on some very practical advice from St. Edith Stein: "And when night comes, and you look back over the day and see how fragmentary everything has been, and how much you planned that has gone undone, and all the reasons you have to be embarrassed and ashamed: just take everything exactly as it is, put it in God's hands and leave it with him."

Leave it with him. Only when we stop trying to accomplish everything ourselves, when we let go of the notion of perfection in prayer, and when we continue to pick ourselves up, recommit, and keep on reconnecting with God can we achieve what before might have felt daunting—the Christian ideal of "constant prayer" as described by St. Paul: "Rejoice always, pray constantly, give thanks in all circumstances; for this is the will of God in Christ Jesus for you" (1 Thes 5:16–18).

Married Life

When asked whether she had ever contemplated divorce, Ruth Graham, late wife of famed preacher Billy Graham, once quipped, "Divorce? No. Murder? Yes."

So I figure it's okay to admit: sometimes I get really angry with my husband. Not just a little annoyed but so angry I can't see straight. And, conversely, of course, there are times when I am the cause of his own version of rage-induced blindness.

Can we talk candidly about married life? I hope so, because nowhere in life is there greater potential for high ideals to come crashing into real-world reality in a burning, flaming mess.

I used to think that happy couples didn't have to work on their marriages. True love is free and easy, right? Actually, wrong.

It doesn't help that our popular culture gets marriage entirely wrong. The world will tell you that you should marry someone who "makes you happy." And then, when that person no longer "makes you happy," you should leave that person and look for a new person who will "make you happy."

I've got news for you. It's not your husband's job to make you happy. Making you happy is God's job alone. Only he can do it. Only God is perfect. No human being will ever make you happy all the time. Even the most virtuous spouse is going to fall short of your expectations sometimes and leave you disappointed.

We already talked about what the word compatible means. To suffer with. Are you ready to suffer with your husband? Glamour magazine wants to know. It might not sound very romantic, but truly being prepared to suffer together and help one another on the way to heaven is what marriage is all about.

Marriage Means Work

The happiest of couples are those who make their marriage a priority and are committed to improving their relationship, in big and small ways, day in and day out. A happy marriage takes work. Lots of work. And a healthy dose of sacrifice too.

Pope Francis recently shared, "How to live a good marriage? United to the Lord, who always renews our love and strengthens it to overcome every difficulty."[8]

There are those pretty words again. It sounds very nice, but how exactly are we to "unite ourselves and our marriages to the Lord?" Even those who are not married are usually called to live together with others, whether it be family members, roommates, brothers or sisters in the religious life, or neighbors. Let's consider some real-world ideas for ways we can work to improve our marriages and our closest relationships.

Give Up Negativity

Do you whine and complain to your husband? Do you criticize and judge too harshly and too quickly? It's okay to admit. Many of us do become comfortable in long-term, committed relationships and fall into the easy habit of venting regular negativity to those who are most often in our presence. Some of this kind of venting can be a normal part of a healthy relationship, but negative

---

8   @Pontifex, March 3, 2014.

words and attitudes tend to feed, grow, spiral out of control, become habitual, and rob you of joy.

Avoid making negative comments and observations. Seek out positive things to say and foster encouraging conversations you can enjoy together.

Be Active Together

What do you and your husband do after the kids have gone to bed or whenever you have downtime together? Do you silently stare at a flickering television screen? Do you retreat to separate corners of the house, each pursuing your own activities?

There is nothing inherently wrong with television or independent projects, but inside of marriage, you have a unique opportunity to replace these things with a shared activity that will feed your friendship and nurture your relationship.

Shared goals and common activities bring you closer and foster a cooperative spirit in your marriage. Think of something the two of you can do together. You might exercise—taking a daily walk is an easy way to connect and engage. You might play board games, plan a summer garden, tackle a home improvement project, or take a class together. The key is to find something you will both enjoy doing together.

Replace some of your daily passivity and separation with an activity you both enjoy. Commit to spending regular time together, focused on common goals, and enjoying one another's company.

Do More Than Your Share

Do you nitpick and keep track of who does what around the house and how often? Do you feel like you are the only one who ever changes the toilet paper roll, empties the dishwasher, takes out the trash, or . . . (fill in this blank with your own pet peeve)?

When you share living space with another adult—especially one of those adults called a husband—it's only human to feel unappreciated on occasion and get annoyed with what sometimes feels like an unfair division of household chores. But the vocation of marriage calls you to be better than that. Stop nitpicking. Stop keeping score. Cheerfully aim to do "more than your share" of household tasks and daily drudgery. Looking for small ways to do "more than your share" is a small sacrifice you can offer up to God, but also a practical means of letting go of the pettiness, selfishness, and bitterness that threaten to poison your married relationship.

Stop keeping track of your husband's daily contributions to household chores. Instead, look for ways to do extra work and take on tasks that are "not your job" with a spirit of cheerful generosity and out of love for our Lord.

Pay More Compliments

Can you think of a time when someone said something critical of you and it cut you to the core? Can you think of a time when someone complimented you and you felt over the moon? Words have real power and are an important tool we can use to build up those we love . . . or tear them down.

Every day of married life presents a challenge for you to use the positive marriage-building power of words. Find something complimentary to say to your spouse every day. Is he stressed about work or worried about the kids? What words can you say to let him know how much you notice and appreciate his dedication and hard work on behalf of your family?

Pay your husband a sincere and specific compliment at least once every day. Look for ways to affirm him as a parent, as a friend, as a worker, and as the most important person in your life.

Pray Together

Some couples avoid praying together because it makes them feel awkward or embarrassed. Others see it as too much of a time commitment. But there is no better way to unite yourself and your marriage to the Lord than by putting yourselves in his presence together.

It doesn't have to be complicated. You might like to pray extemporaneously together, but if that's not your style, simply praying a Hail Mary together before going to sleep at night or praying the Angelus in the morning can be beautiful ways to unite your hearts in prayer. You might also try reading Scripture together. Choose a Psalm or a Gospel passage to read aloud and then share what is on your hearts with each other and with God. Just this one small practice can help you not only grow closer to God but get to know your husband on a whole new spiritual level. Shared spirituality is an intimacy every couple deserves to experience.

Set aside time to pray with your spouse every day. Overcome any personal reluctance you might have and commit to praying with and for your husband on a daily basis.

Soak Up the Sacraments

We have such a great gift in the sacraments! Because he loves us, Jesus gave us the sacraments as a means of attaining the grace we need to do God's will every day. The sacraments feed our souls, heal us, and fill us with God's own life.

This all sounds lovely, but how often do we take the sacraments for granted? Do we remember that our marriage itself is a sacrament and ask God to give us the graces we need to grow in love together?

Do we receive the Eucharist unthinkingly and avoid confession?

Challenge yourself to find new ways to partake in the sacraments with your husband. You might make time for a weekly Holy Hour together, attend an extra Mass per week, or have a "confession date" followed by dinner out. Find a way to put yourself and your husband in God's presence more often and you will find yourselves growing closer to one another as you grow in love for God.

Find new ways to receive and appreciate the sacraments together. Pray daily for the sacramental grace from your marriage and look for opportunities to receive the Eucharist and sacrament of Penance together.

Speak Healing Words

Pope Francis recently encouraged engaged couples to use the healing words "please," "thank you," and "I'm sorry."

These are everyday words we often use with others but sometimes neglect to use enough with those we love most. We should think about the healing power of everyday words and use them to build our marriages and communicate love, appreciation, and humility to our spouses.

Use the word please to soften the everyday demands of life and the ongoing requests we all make of each other in marriage. Think of some thankless task your husband does for you on a regular basis (making dinner, emptying the trash, doing laundry, going to work, cleaning the gutters?) and look for a way to say thank you for his gift of service. Be quick to notice even small offenses you may be guilty of in your relationship, and offer a genuine apology for them. We all long to hear healing words, and yet sometimes fall into the bad habit of neglecting to say them or thinking "he knows that already."

Use healing words (please, thank you, I'm sorry, and I love you) every day. Look for new opportunities to love, appreciate, thank, heal, and build up your husband through small words and phrases.

Only your husband knows, in terrifying detail, your glaring weaknesses and glorious strengths. Only your husband can see the worst of your flaws and choose to love you anyway. Only your husband, in spite of your weakness and his, can focus on the woman God wants you to be and call on you to be that woman.

Inside of marriage, and indeed inside all of our closest family relationships, God calls on us to do the small, meaningful things, which are often the hardest things to do. Say you're sorry. Offer forgiveness. Hold your tongue. Smile when you don't want to. Do the thing that's so unfair you should not—do you hear me, you should NOT—have to do it.

Your married life is beautiful and must be protected. Do the small thing. Do the hard thing. Begin anew.

Balancing Work and Family Life

"Tell me what to do!" a young mom emailed me once. "I feel like I'm drowning in a sea of important things. With so many work and family obligations, it's hard for me to know where I should focus my time and energy. I wind up trying to do everything at once and feeling like a mess."

No matter your state in life, we all do struggle sometimes to find balance among our priorities. If you work, the demands of your job threaten to take over your life in unhealthy ways. If you have a family, your husband, and especially children, lay claim to every last bit of time and energy you can possibly spare. And then they take a little more.

We are doing many things, and we are good at doing many things. The female brain is amazing in its capacity for thinking in a fluid stream, seamlessly intertwining all variety of thoughts and activities as we move throughout our days. This feminine way of thinking is different from a masculine approach, which is much more linear.

We might think, "I need to sweep that floor. Oh! I think maybe the baby is waking up from her nap. I wonder if it stopped raining outside. I must call that client back. Gee, my nails could sure use a fresh coat of polish. Did I remember to take the meat out of the freezer for dinner tonight?"

A man, however, might think, "I need to sweep that floor," and then he would sweep the floor before moving on to the next thought and action. I do not understand this single-minded approach to life at all, but my husband assures me that it's real.

Of course, our capacity for attention to multiple thoughts and details is a great gift that women have, in that we can use this skill to accomplish many things and care for small details that might otherwise go unnoticed. We've already considered the fact that the small details of our days build the relationships where we find true meaning, value, and purpose in our lives. It's in noticing and attending to the smallest of needs that we can make others feel known and truly loved.

But our attention to multiple thoughts and details can also be exhausting. Uncontrolled and unbalanced, a scattered flow of thoughts, ideas, and actions will leave us feeling drained, depleted, and like we are failing at everything.

Whether you are balancing caring for aging parents and full-time work, a toddler's demands and a new pregnancy, running a household and working part-time from home, or any combination of obligations, you need a plan. You need some structure in your days to give yourself freedom to focus on doing just one thing at a time. When it comes to making a schedule for yourself, it is helpful to keep some basic principles in mind.

Know That You Get to Choose

You are not a victim of your life. No matter what is going on, and no matter how trying your current circumstances are, every one of us has the responsibility to choose how we will spend our time. Your obligations might leave you with little flexibility in your schedule, but that does not excuse you from the responsibility of intentionally deciding how you will spend your time.

I remember talking to my sister on the phone years ago when I was a mom of many small children, and I felt like I was barely keeping up.

"I feel like life just happens to me," I told her. "I get up every morning and just start responding to things."

Well, that is no kind of plan. In fact, accepting that "life just happens to me" is a recipe for frustration and unhappiness. Without an intentional plan for how you will spend your time, you always will come away feeling like a failure. With no clear goal in mind, you will never meet your goals or accomplish the things that are important to you.

Of course, I understand seasons of chaos in life. I have lived through my fair share of weeks and even months where it felt like I deserved a medal just for putting on a "not-as-dirty-as the-other-ones" t-shirt, combing my hair, and brushing my teeth.

Seasons of chaos, whether brought on by illness, pregnancy, work, or some other unpreventable crisis, should be just that, however: seasons. With an end in sight. Chaos should never be a way of life. You have responsibility for your life, and you get to decide how you will spend your time.

Think About Your Priorities

Take time to think about what things are important to you and how much time you think you should reasonably spend on each of them on a regular basis. Write them down! Important general areas of focus for many women include spiritual life, work (at home or in the workplace), marriage, children, and self.

Once you have a list of what your priorities are, and how much time you think you should be spending on each, it's time to find out how you actually do spend your time each day. Keep track of yourself throughout a typical day and notice where you really do spend your time. This can be an eye-opening and humbling exercise.

What distracts you from your priorities? Technology is a common obstacle in our quest to focus on what's truly important. We check email on our phone, and then the next thing we know thirty minutes have passed and the only thing we have accomplished is scrolling through mindless videos on social media.

If technology is a problem for you, relegate your use of your phone or computer to only certain controlled times in your day, or decide that there will be time each day where you turn your phone off and focus on other things. Whatever your distractions are, take note of them and come up with a way to minimize or eliminate them.

Once you have dealt with distractions, then you need a schedule. Whether you are an at-home mom or a busy executive, you need a plan. We do not all love to schedule things, and what you decide for your daily schedule can be as rigid or as flexible as you like. Your daily or weekly plan can be a formal, written schedule and calendar, or it can be an informal one you simply keep in your mind. (E.g., "Tuesdays are when I catch up on laundry"; "I answer emails for fifteen minutes in the afternoon"; or "I spend time with the kids, helping with homework each night after dinner.") Figure out what works for you, and then (here is the key!) . . . do it.

Start Now

Too often, we put off what we see as the painful process of getting organized and being intentional about how we spend our time. It feels easier simply to slide through life thinking you'll be more organized and intentional when the kids are grown or when you get your dream job, or when your husband retires.

But we are not called to live in the future. We are called to live out our vocations as women right now, today, and every day, to the best of our abilities.

Do not let a "perfect" idea of what your daily life should look like become the enemy of the "good" you could be accomplishing by beginning to take responsibility for how you spend your time, starting right now. "Yesterday is gone. Tomorrow has not yet come. We have only today. Let us begin."[9]

Spirit of Hospitality

Do you love the story of Mary and Martha in the Bible? I think we all do, because we all are Mary and Martha, to some extent. We understand this conflict.

> Now as they went on their way, he entered a village; and a woman named Martha received him into her house. And she had a sister called Mary, who sat at the Lord's feet and listened to his teaching. But Martha was distracted with much serving; and she went to him and said, "Lord, do you not care that my sister has left me to serve alone? Tell her then to help me." But the Lord answered her,

---

9   Mother Teresa, *Where There Is Love, There Is God: A Path to Closer Union with God and Greater Love for Others* (New York: Image, 2010) 191.

"Martha, Martha, you are anxious and troubled about many things; one thing is needful. Mary has chosen the good portion, which shall not be taken away from her." (Lk 10:38–42)

This Gospel story is precious to women because it is such an endearing study of the interior conflict so many of us face when attempting to balance our priorities. Have you ever hosted an event where you got so stressed and distracted by the details of the work you neglected to connect with your guests? Making such a mistake, as Martha did, highlights for us the truth that our relationships with others are more important than things. People are more important than work.

Women have a natural gift of hospitality. That does not mean that we are all like Martha Stewart in our ability to pull off a perfect Easter brunch; it means, as outlined earlier, that we have feminine gifts of receptivity, sensitivity, compassion, beauty, and generosity that enable us to serve others and make them feel welcome.

Note that, in this passage, we read that Martha "received [Jesus] into her house." She then becomes distracted with pots and pans, and possibly a roast in the oven, but she begins by receiving Jesus. Receiving others is what we women do. We do it well, and we do it in many ways.

Jesus knew this when he chose to reveal his true identity to the Samaritan woman at the well whom we read about in the Gospel of John. As a gentle way of introducing himself, a foreign man, to the Samaritan woman, he appeals to her feminine spirit of hospitality: "Jesus said to her, 'Give me a drink'" (Jn 4:7).

Give me a drink. And so begins an unlikely conversation that would change the course of the Samaritan woman's life forever.

"One Thing Is Needful"

Jesus knew too that Martha was practicing the feminine gift of hospitality when he spent time in her home and she got lost among the dishes. I love how in the conversation we read in the Gospel, Martha is so sure that she is correct in her anger against her sister that she bosses Jesus: "Tell her to help me!"

Imagine her surprise then, when Jesus does not do as she says, but instead reprimands her for her distraction from the one important thing. And what is that one important thing? It's Jesus, of course. Jesus loves Martha so much, even in her distraction, that he challenges her very gently, saying her name two times and calls on her to pay attention to what truly matters.

It can be easy for us to read a story like this one and think it's obvious that Martha should have been focused on Jesus. I mean, really, Jesus was in her living room. Martha was so busy in the kitchen that she was missing out on Jesus in her living room!

And yet, how many of us do exactly that? Jesus may not be knocking on your door, asking to come in and spend time chatting at the kitchen table, but Jesus is present to you in many ways throughout your busy life, in the form of people. Relationships with people, and with Jesus, whom we meet in others, are more important than any work we might ever do.

The work we women do in our homes, in our kitchens, in our churches, in our schools, and in our communities is vital and important stuff. Women do so many good things for their families and the world at large through their natural gift of hospitality, but Jesus's words to Martha remind us that our value and our worth come not from anything we might ever do. Our worth comes from who we are: beloved daughters of God. God wants a real relationship with each of us, a deep and personal connection that has value far beyond any Easter brunch we might ever host.

Satan's Lies

Remember the serpent in the Garden of Eden? The one who told lies to tempt Eve at the very beginning of the human story? That serpent is still around; he is still telling lies, and he targets women in a special way. God predicted this when he pronounced judgement against the serpent after the first sin: "I will put enmity between you and the woman, and between your seed and her seed; he shall bruise your head, and you shall bruise his heel" (Gn 3:15).

There is indeed enmity between Satan and women. We have already considered the ways in which Mary's obedient yes enabled the redemption of Eve's disobedient no. Mary's full embrace of all that God was calling her to be, as a mother and as a daughter of God, enabled the salvation of man and our freedom from sin, a devastating fact for the Evil One. A woman who knows who she is and who is open to the will of God is a powerful force for the good.

Satan knows this.

Do you remember the glimmer of hope Adam saw in Eve, even as they were surrounded by the shame and sorrow of their sin? It was the hope that Eve would be "the mother of all living," the hope that all women represent with our capacity for self-giving, life-giving love. Satan sees that hope in women too. There is no force on earth Satan fears more than the power of a faithful woman who knows who she is and embraces her womanly vocation of love.

The Subtle Serpent

It is because he fears our strength that Satan tells us lies. In Genesis, we read, "Now the

serpent was more subtle than any other wild creature that the Lord God had made" (Gn 3:1).

And Satan still is subtle. You may not see him as
a serpent slithering around your feet in the garden,
but we all do sometimes hear his quiet voice chal-
lenging our identity as daughters of God, worthy of
loving and being loved. It is a voice that tempts us
to distrust God, as Eve did, when she believed God
would not give her good things. It is a voice that distracts us with jealousy and competition when we
see the good things others have. It is a voice that
tells us that only a fool would make a gift of herself,
only a sucker would find fulfillment in loving and
serving others. It is a voice that tells us in order to
be truly liberated and happy, we must squash our
inclination to love and nurture, and we must free
ourselves from our capacity to bring forth new life,
both physically and spiritually.

It is a voice that tells us that, no matter how hard
we try, we will never be good enough, beautiful
enough, or worthy enough for God's love.

But we get to choose. We get to decide if we will
listen to the voice of the serpent or if we will seek
out and listen to God's plan for our lives. We can
recognize the enmity that exists between us and
the serpent and reject Satan's lies—lies that he tells
out of fear of the goodness and strength he sees in
us. We can learn to recognize that womanly goodness and strength in ourselves, and to embrace
our unique calling. The world—filled with pain,

sorrow, confusion, and sin as it is—needs us to do exactly that.

"The world doesn't need what women have; it needs what women are."[10]

Be Who You Are

God calls you to be a saint, and your calling is not one you can step into half-heartedly. Take courage. Speak truth to Satan's lies. Allow God's truth, about who you are and what you were made for, to permeate your body and soul. Allow God's words about his great love for you and Mary's example of womanly virtue to sit in your heart until you can begin to absorb their awesome strength.

You are woman, and you are worthy. God calls you to greatness through your unique feminine vocation of love. He has given you gifts of receptivity, sensitivity, compassion, beauty, and generosity to fulfill that calling, but no one can answer your own personal call to life-giving love but you.

Part of the beauty and joy of authentic womanhood is that it is expressed differently in each of us. We have many gifts and strengths in common, but God loves each of us with a unique and personal love, and he calls each of us to a particular

---

10 Edith Stein in Leah Darrow, *The Other Side of Beauty: Embracing God's Vision for Love and True Worth* (Nashville: Thomas Nelson, 2017) 17.

mission—one that only you can know and only you can answer.

Do you know uniquely strong, sensitive, beautiful women? Do they know just how uniquely strong, sensitive, and beautiful they are? Do you know how uniquely strong, sensitive, and beautiful you are?

Most of us don't, and it's time we found out.

What joys might we find in using our own feminine gifts to celebrate and encourage those same gifts in others? What kind of satisfaction might we find in imitating Mary's example and answering our call to self-giving, life-giving love by using our feminine strengths to build up Christ's kingdom on earth?

Let's find out together. Let us begin.

PART TWO

Wisdom and Prayers for Women

7

WISDOM OF THE CHURCH

FROM THE CATECHISM

The Domestic Church

hrist chose to be born and grow up in the bosom of the holy family of Joseph and Mary. The Church is nothing other than "the family of God." From the beginning, the core of the Church was often constituted by those who had become believers "together with all [their] household" (Acts 18:8). When they were converted, they desired that "their whole household" should also be saved (Acts 11:14; 16:31). These families who became believers were islands of Christian life in an unbelieving world.

In our own time, in a world often alien and even hostile to faith, believing families are of primary importance as centers of living, radiant faith. For this reason the Second Vatican Council, using an ancient expression, calls the family the Ecclesia domestica (LG 11; cf. FC 21). It is in the bosom of the family that parents are "by word and example . . .

77

the first heralds of the faith with regard to their children. They should encourage them in the vocation which is proper to each child, fostering with special care any religious vocation" (LG 11).

It is here that the father of the family, the mother, children, and all members of the family exercise the priesthood of the baptized in a privileged way "by the reception of the sacraments, prayer and thanksgiving, the witness of a holy life, and self-denial and active charity" (LG 10). Thus the home is the first school of Christian life and "a school for human enrichment" (GS 52 § 1). Here one learns endurance and the joy of work, fraternal love, generous—even repeated—forgiveness, and above all divine worship in prayer and the offering of one's life.

We must also remember the great number of single persons who, because of the particular circumstances in which they have to live—often not of their choosing—are especially close to Jesus' heart and therefore deserve the special affection and active solicitude of the Church, especially of pastors. Many remain without a human family often due to conditions of poverty. Some live their situation in the spirit of the Beatitudes, serving God and neighbor in exemplary fashion. The doors of homes, the "domestic churches," and of the great family which is the Church must be open to all of them. "No one is without a family in this world: the

Church is a home and family for everyone, especially those who 'labor and are heavy laden'" (FC 85; cf. Mt 11:28).[11]

The Nature of the Family

The conjugal community is established upon the consent of the spouses. Marriage and the family are ordered to the good of the spouses and to the procreation and education of children. The love of the spouses and the begetting of children create among members of the same family personal relationships and primordial responsibilities.

A man and a woman united in marriage, together with their children, form a family. This institution is prior to any recognition by public authority, which has an obligation to recognize it. It should be considered the normal reference point by which the different forms of family relationship are to be evaluated.

In creating man and woman, God instituted the human family and endowed it with its fundamental constitution. Its members are persons equal in dignity. For the common good of its members and of society, the family necessarily has manifold responsibilities, rights, and duties.[12]

---

11 *Catechism of the Catholic Church*, nos. 1655–58.
12 Ibid., nos. 2201–3.

The Christian Family

" The Christian family constitutes a specific revelation and realization of ecclesial communion, and for this reason it can and should be called a domestic church" (FC 21; cf. LG 11). It is a community of faith, hope, and charity; it assumes singular importance in the Church, as is evident in the New Testament (Eph 5:21b: 4; Col 3:18-21; 1 Pet 3:1-7).

The Christian family is a communion of persons, a sign and image of the communion of the Father and the Son in the Holy Spirit. In the procreation and education of children it reflects the Father's work of creation. It is called to partake of the prayer and sacrifice of Christ. Daily prayer and the reading of the Word of God strengthen it in charity. The Christian family has an evangelizing and missionary task.

The relationships within the family bring an affinity of feelings, affections and interests, arising above all from the members' respect for one another. The family is a privileged community called to achieve a "sharing of thought and common deliberation by the spouses as well as their eager cooperation as parents in the children's upbringing" (GS 52 § 1).[13]

---

13 Ibid., nos. 2204–6.

From the Compendium of the Catechism

Honor Your Father and Your Mother

459. What are the duties of children toward their parents?

Children owe respect (filial piety), gratitude, docility and obedience to their parents. In paying them respect and in fostering good relationships with their brothers and sisters, children contribute to the growth in harmony and holiness in family life in general. Adult children should give their parents material and moral support whenever they find themselves in situations of distress, sickness, loneliness, or old age.[14]

460. What are the duties of parents toward their children?

Parents, in virtue of their participation in the fatherhood of God, have the first responsibility for the education of their children and they are the first heralds of the faith for them. They have the duty to love and respect their children as persons and as children of God and to provide, as far as is possible, for their physical and spiritual needs. They should select for them a suitable school and help them with prudent counsel in the choice of

---

14 See CCC 2214–20; 2251.

their profession and their state of life. In particular they have the mission of educating their children in the Christian faith.[15]

You Shall Not Kill

472. Why must society protect every embryo?

The inalienable right to life of every human individual from the first moment of conception is a constitutive element of civil society and its legislation. When the State does not place its power at the service of the rights of all and in particular of the more vulnerable, including unborn children, the very foundations of a State based on law are undermined.[16]

474. What duty do we have toward our body?

We must take reasonable care of our own physical health and that of others but avoid the cult of the body and every kind of excess. Also to be avoided are the use of drugs which cause very serious damage to human health and life, as well as the abuse of food, alcohol, tobacco and medicine.[17]

---

15 See CCC 2221–31.
16 See CCC 2273–74.
17 See CCC 2288–91.

You Shall Not Commit Adultery

491. In what way is everyone called to live chastity?

As followers of Christ, the model of all chastity, all the baptised are called to live chastely in keeping with their particular states of life. Some profess virginity or consecrated celibacy which enables them to give themselves to God alone with an undivided heart in a remarkable manner. Others, if they are married live in conjugal chastity, or if unmarried practise chastity in continence.[18]

495. What are the goods of conjugal love to which sexuality is ordered?

The goods of conjugal love, which for those who are baptized is sanctified by the sacrament of Matrimony, are unity, fidelity, indissolubility, and an openness to the procreation of life.[19]

496. What is the meaning of the conjugal act?

The conjugal act has a twofold meaning: unitive (the mutual self-giving of the spouses) and procreative (an openness to the transmission of life). No one may break the inseparable connection which God has established between these two

---

18 See CCC 2348–50; 2394.
19 See CCC 2360–61; 2397–98.

meanings of the conjugal act by excluding one or the other of them.[20]

497. When is it moral to regulate births?

The regulation of births, which is an aspect of responsible fatherhood and motherhood, is objectively morally acceptable when it is pursued by the spouses without external pressure; when it is practiced not out of selfishness but for serious reasons; and with methods that conform to the objective criteria of morality, that is, periodic continence and use of the infertile periods.[21]

498. What are immoral means of birth control?

Every action—for example, direct sterilization or contraception—is intrinsically immoral which (either in anticipation of the conjugal act, in its accomplishment or in the development of its natural consequences) proposes, as an end or as a means, to hinder procreation.[22]

500. How should children be considered?

A child is a gift of God, the supreme gift of marriage. There is no such thing as a right to have children (e.g. "a child at any cost"). But a child does have the right to be the fruit of the conjugal act

---

20 See CCC 2362–67.
21 See CCC 2368–69; 2399.
22 See CCC 2370–72.

of its parents as well as the right to be respected as a person from the moment of conception.[23]

501. What can spouses do when they do not have children?

Should the gift of a child not be given to them, after exhausting all legitimate medical options, spouses can show their generosity by way of foster care or adoption or by performing meaningful services for others. In this way they realize a precious spiritual fruitfulness.[24]

Prayer in the Christian Life

534. What is prayer?

Prayer is the raising of one's mind and heart to God, or the petition of good things from him in accord with his will. It is always the gift of God who comes to encounter man. Christian prayer is the personal and living relationship of the children of God with their Father who is infinitely good, with his Son Jesus Christ, and with the Holy Spirit who dwells in their hearts.[25]

---

23 See CCC 2378.
24 See CCC 2379.
25 See CCC 2558–65; 2590.

542. When did Jesus pray?

The Gospel often shows Jesus at prayer. We see him draw apart to pray in solitude, even at night. He prays before the decisive moments of his mission or that of his apostles. In fact, all his life is a prayer because he is in a constant communion of love with the Father.[26]

546. How did the Virgin Mary pray?

Mary's prayer was characterized by faith and by the generous offering of her whole being to God. The Mother of Jesus is also the new Eve, the "Mother of all the living". She prays to Jesus for the needs of all people.[27]

547. Is there a prayer of Mary in the Gospel?

Along with the prayer of Mary at Cana in Galilee, the Gospel gives us the Magnificat (Luke 1:46-55) which is the song both of the Mother of God and of the Church, the joyous thanksgiving that rises from the hearts of the poor because their hope is met by the fulfillment of the divine promises.[28]

---

26 See CCC 2600–4; 2620.
27 See CCC 2617, 2618, 2622, 2674, 2679.
28 See CCC 2619.

PAPAL DOCUMENTS AND TEACHING ON WOMEN

On the Dignity of Women

As you know, the Church is proud to have glorified and liberated woman, and in the course of the centuries, in diversity of characters, to have brought into relief her basic equality with man. But the hour is coming, in fact has come, when the vocation of woman is being achieved in its fullness, the hour in which woman acquires in the world an influence, an effect and a power never hitherto achieved. That is why, at this moment when the human race is under-going so deep a transformation, women impregnated with the spirit of the Gospel can do so much to aid mankind in not falling. . . .

You women have always had as your lot the protection of the home, the love of beginnings and an understanding of cradles. You are present in the mystery of a life beginning. You offer consolation in the departure of death. Our technology runs the risk of becoming inhuman. Reconcile men with life and above all, we beseech you, watch carefully over the future of our race. Hold back the hand of man who, in a moment of folly, might attempt to destroy human civilization.

Wives, mothers of families, the first educators of the human race in the intimacy of the family circle, pass on to your sons and your daughters the traditions of your fathers at the same time that you prepare them for an unsearchable future. Always remember that by her children a mother belongs to that future which perhaps she will not see. . . . Women, you do know how to make truth sweet, tender and accessible; make it your task to bring the spirit of this council into institutions, schools, homes and daily life. Women of the entire universe, whether Christian or non-believing, you to whom life is entrusted at this grave moment in history, it is for you to save the peace of the world.[29]

POPE ST. PAUL VI

Since "the Church is in Christ as a sacrament . . . of intimate union with God and of the unity of the whole human race", the special presence of the Mother of God in the mystery of the Church makes us think of the exceptional link between this "woman" and the whole human family. It is a question here of every man and woman, all the sons and daughters of the human race, in whom from generation to generation a fundamental inheritance is realized, the inheritance that belongs to all humanity and that is linked with the mystery of the

29 Pope Saint Paul VI, *Message of the Council to Women* (1965).

biblical "beginning": "God created man in his own image, in the image of God he created him; male and female he created them"(Gen 1:27).

This eternal truth about the human being, man and woman—a truth which is immutably fixed in human experience—at the same time constitutes the mystery which only in "the Incarnate Word takes on light . . . (since) Christ fully reveals man to himself and makes his supreme calling clear", as the Council teaches. In this "revealing of man to himself", do we not need to find a special place for that "woman" who was the Mother of Christ? Cannot the "message" of Christ, contained in the Gospel, which has as its background the whole of Scripture, both the Old and the New Testament, say much to the Church and to humanity about the dignity of women and their vocation?[30]

POPE ST. JOHN PAUL II

———

Therefore the Church gives thanks for each and every woman: for mothers, for sisters, for wives; for women consecrated to God in virginity; for women dedicated to the many human beings who await the gratuitous love of another person; for women who watch over the human persons in the family, which is the fundamental sign of the human community; for women who work professionally, and who at

---

30 Pope Saint John Paul II, Apostolic Letter *Mulieris Dignitatem* (1998).

times are burdened by a great social responsibility; for "perfect" women and for "weak" women—for all women as they have come forth from the heart of God in all the beauty and richness of their femininity; as they have been embraced by his eternal love; as, together with men, they are pilgrims on this earth, which is the temporal "homeland" of all people and is transformed sometimes into a "valley of tears"; as they assume, together with men, a common responsibility for the destiny of humanity according to daily necessities and according to that definitive destiny which the human family has in God himself, in the bosom of the ineffable Trinity.[31]

POPE ST. JOHN PAUL II

Priscilla and Aquila: The Apostolic Commitment of Families

Hence, we come to know the most important role that this couple played in the environment of the primitive Church: that of welcoming in their own house the group of local Christians when they gathered to listen to the Word of God and to celebrate the Eucharist. . . . One thing is sure: together with the gratitude of the early Church, of which St. Paul speaks, we must also add our own, since thanks to the faith and apostolic commitment of the lay faithful, of families, of spouses like

---

31 Ibid.

Priscilla and Aquila, Christianity has reached our generation.

It could grow not only thanks to the Apostles who announced it. In order to take root in people's land and develop actively, the commitment of these families, these spouses, these Christian communities, of these lay faithful was necessary in order to offer the "humus" for the growth of the faith. As always, it is only in this way that the Church grows.

This couple in particular demonstrates how important the action of Christian spouses is. When they are supported by the faith and by a strong spirituality, their courageous commitment for the Church and in the Church becomes natural. The daily sharing of their life prolongs and in some way is sublimated in the assuming of a common responsibility in favor of the Mystical Body of Christ, even if just a little part of it. Thus it was in the first generation and thus it will often be.

A further lesson we cannot neglect to draw from their example: every home can transform itself into a little church. Not only in the sense that in them must reign the typical Christian love made of altruism and of reciprocal care, but still more in the sense that the whole of family life, based on faith, is called to revolve around the singular lordship of Jesus Christ.[32]

POPE BENEDICT XVI

---

32 Pope Benedict XVI, "General Audience, Priscilla and Aquila"

The Special Importance of Women in Evangelization

Today, we have come to the end of our journey among the witnesses of early Christianity mentioned in the New Testament writings. And we use the last step of this first journey to dedicate our attention to the many female figures who played an effective and precious role in spreading the Gospel.

In conformity with what Jesus himself said of the woman who anointed his head shortly before the Passion: "Truly, I say to you, wherever this Gospel is preached in the whole world, what she has done will be told in memory of her" (Mt 26: 13; Mk 14: 9), their testimony cannot be forgotten.[33]

POPE BENEDICT XVI

Women as Disciples of Christ

In addition to the Twelve, pillars of the Church and fathers of the new People of God, many women were also chosen to number among the disciples. I can only mention very briefly those who followed Jesus himself, beginning with the Prophetess

(The Holy See, February 7, 2007), http://w2.vatican.va/content/benedict-xvi/en/audiences/2007/documents/hf_ben-xvi_aud_20070207.html.

33 Pope Benedict XVI, "General Audience, Women at the Service of the Gospel" (The Holy See, February 14, 2007), http://w2.vatican.va/content/benedict-xvi/en/audiences/2007/documents/hf_ben-xvi_aud_20070214.html.

Anna (cf. Lk 2:36-38), to the Samaritan woman (cf. Jn 4:1-39), the Syro-Phoenician woman (cf. Mk 7:24-30), the woman with the hemorrhage (cf. Mt 9:20-22) and the sinful woman whose sins were forgiven (cf. Lk 7:36-50).

I will not even refer to the protagonists of some of his effective parables, for example, the housewife who made bread (cf. Mt 13:33), the woman who lost the drachma (cf. Lk 15:8-10), the widow who pestered the judge (cf. Lk 18:1-8). More important for our topic are the women who played an active role in the context of Jesus' mission.

In the first place, we think spontaneously of the Virgin Mary, who with her faith and maternal labors collaborated in a unique way in our Redemption to the point that Elizabeth proclaimed her "Blessed . . . among women" (Lk 1:42), adding: "Blessed is she who believed . . ." (Lk 1:45). . . .

Then there are various women with roles of responsibility who gravitated in their different capacities around the figure of Jesus. The women who followed Jesus to assist him with their own means, some of whose names Luke has passed down to us, are an eloquent example: Mary of Magdala, Joanna, Susanna and "many others" (cf. Lk 8:2-3).

The Gospels then tell us that the women, unlike the Twelve, did not abandon Jesus in the hour of his Passion (cf. Mt 27:56, 61; Mk 15:40). Among them, Mary Magdalene stands out in particular. Not only was she present at the Passion, but she was also the first witness and herald of the Risen One (cf. Jn 20:1, 11-18).

It was precisely to Mary Magdalene that St. Thomas Aquinas reserved the special title, "Apostle of the Apostles" (apostolorum apostola), dedicating to her this beautiful comment: "Just as a woman had announced the words of death to the first man, so also a woman was the first to announce to the Apostles the words of life" (Super Ioannem, ed. Cai, 2519). . . .

Nor was the female presence in the sphere of the primitive Church in any way secondary. . . . It is rather to St. Paul that we are indebted for a more ample documentation on the dignity and ecclesial role of women. He begins with the fundamental principle according to which for the baptized: "There is neither Jew nor Greek, there is neither slave nor free, there is neither male nor female; for you are all one in Christ Jesus" (Gal 3:28), that is, all are united in the same basic dignity, although each with specific functions (cf. I Cor 12: 27: 30).

The Apostle accepts as normal the fact that a woman can "prophesy" in the Christian community (1 Cor 11:5), that is, speak openly under the influence of the Spirit, as long as it is for the edification of the community and done in a dignified manner. . . .

In short, without the generous contribution of many women, the history of Christianity would have developed very differently.[34]

POPE BENEDICT XVI

The Situation of the Family in the World Today

The situation in which the family finds itself presents positive and negative aspects: the first are a sign of the salvation of Christ operating in the world; the second, a sign of the refusal that man gives to the love of God.

On the one hand, in fact, there is a more lively awareness of personal freedom and greater attention to the quality of interpersonal relationships in marriage, to promoting the dignity of women, to responsible procreation, to the education of children. There is also an awareness of the need for the development of interfamily relationships, for reciprocal spiritual and material assistance, the rediscovery of the ecclesial mission proper to the family and its responsibility for the building of a more just society. On the other hand, however, signs are not lacking of a disturbing degradation of some fundamental values: a mistaken theoretical and practical concept of the independence of the spouses in relation to each other; serious misconceptions

---

34 Ibid.

regarding the relationship of authority between parents and children; the concrete difficulties that the family itself experiences in the transmission of values; the growing number of divorces; the scourge of abortion; the ever more frequent recourse to sterilization; the appearance of a truly contraceptive mentality.

At the root of these negative phenomena there frequently lies a corruption of the idea and the experience of freedom, conceived not as a capacity for realizing the truth of God's plan for marriage and the family, but as an autonomous power of self-affirmation, often against others, for one's own selfish well-being.[35]

POPE ST. JOHN PAUL II

Total Gift of Self in Marriage

Christian revelation recognizes two specific ways of realizing the vocation of the human person in its entirety, to love: marriage and virginity or celibacy. Either one is, in its own proper form, an actuation of the most profound truth of man, of his being "created in the image of God."

Consequently, sexuality, by means of which man and woman give themselves to one another through the acts which are proper and exclusive to spouses,

---

35 Pope Saint John Paul II, Apostolic Exhortation *Familiaris Consortio* (1981), no. 6.

is by no means something purely biological, but concerns the innermost being of the human person as such. It is realized in a truly human way only if it is an integral part of the love by which a man and a woman commit themselves totally to one another until death. The total physical self-giving would be a lie if it were not the sign and fruit of a total personal self-giving, in which the whole person, including the temporal dimension, is present: if the person were to withhold something or reserve the possibility of deciding otherwise in the future, by this very fact he or she would not be giving totally.

This totality which is required by conjugal love also corresponds to the demands of responsible fertility. This fertility is directed to the generation of a human being, and so by its nature it surpasses the purely biological order and involves a whole series of personal values. For the harmonious growth of these values a persevering and unified contribution by both parents is necessary.

The only "place" in which this self-giving in its whole truth is made possible is marriage, the covenant of conjugal love freely and consciously chosen, whereby man and woman accept the intimate community of life and love willed by God Himself which only in this light manifests its true meaning. The institution of marriage is not an undue interference by society or authority, nor the extrinsic imposition of a form. Rather it is an interior requirement of the covenant of conjugal love which is publicly affirmed as unique and exclusive, in order to live in complete fidelity to the plan of God, the Creator. A person's freedom, far from being restricted by this fidelity, is secured against every form of subjectivism or relativism and is made a sharer in creative Wisdom.[36]

POPE ST. JOHN PAUL II

Marriage, Virginity, Celibacy

Virginity or celibacy for the sake of the Kingdom of God not only does not contradict the dignity of marriage but presupposes it and confirms it. Marriage and virginity or celibacy are two ways of expressing and living the one mystery of the covenant of God with His people. When marriage is not esteemed, neither can consecrated virginity or celibacy exist; when human sexuality is not regarded as a great value given by the Creator, the renunciation of it for the sake of the Kingdom of Heaven loses its meaning. . . .

In virginity or celibacy, the human being is awaiting, also in a bodily way, the eschatological marriage of Christ with the Church, giving himself or herself completely to the Church in the hope that Christ may give Himself to the Church in the full truth of eternal life. The celibate person thus anticipates in his or her flesh the new world of the future resurrection.

---

36 Ibid., no. 11.

By virtue of this witness, virginity or celibacy keeps alive in the Church a consciousness of the mystery of marriage and defends it from any reduction and impoverishment.

Virginity or celibacy, by liberating the human heart in a unique way, "so as to make it burn with greater love for God and all humanity," bears witness that the Kingdom of God and His justice is that pearl of great price which is preferred to every other value no matter how great, and hence must be sought as the only definitive value. It is for this reason that the Church, throughout her history, has always defended the superiority of this charism to that of marriage, by reason of the wholly singular link which it has with the Kingdom of God.

In spite of having renounced physical fecundity, the celibate person becomes spiritually fruitful, the father and mother of many, cooperating in the realization of the family according to God's plan.

Christian couples therefore have the right to expect from celibate persons a good example and a witness of fidelity to their vocation until death. Just as fidelity at times becomes difficult for married people and requires sacrifice, mortification and self-denial, the same can happen to celibate persons, and their fidelity, even in the trials that may occur, should strengthen the fidelity of married couples.

These reflections on virginity or celibacy can enlighten and help those who, for reasons

independent of their own will, have been unable to
marry and have then accepted their situation in a
spirit of service.[37]

PONE ST. JOHN PAUL II

There is a truly marvellous design inherent in
the Sacrament of Matrimony! And it unfolds in the
simplicity and frailty of the human condition. We
are well aware of how many difficulties two spouses
experience. . . . The important thing is to keep alive
their bond with God, who stands as the foundation
of the marital bond. And the true bond is always the
Lord. When the family prays, the bond is preserved.
When the husband prays for his wife and the wife
prays for her husband, that bond becomes strong;
one praying for the other. It is true that there are
so many difficulties in married life, so many, when
there is insufficient work or money, when the children have problems. So much to contend with.
And many times the husband and wife become
a little fractious and argue between themselves.
They argue, this is how it is, there is always arguing in marriage, sometimes the plates even fly. Yet
we must not become saddened by this, this is the
human condition. The secret is that love is stronger than the moment when there is arguing, and
therefore I always advise spouses: do not let a day

---

37 Ibid., no. 16.

when you have argued end without making peace. Always![38]

POPE FRANCIS

The Sanctity of Marriage

Christian spouses, in virtue of the sacrament of Matrimony, whereby they signify and partake of the mystery of that unity and fruitful love which exists between Christ and His Church, help each other to attain to holiness in their married life and in the rearing and education of their children. By reason of their state and rank in life they have their own special gift among the people of God. From the wedlock of Christians there comes the family, in which new citizens of human society are born, who by the grace of the Holy Spirit received in baptism are made children of God, thus perpetuating the people of God through the centuries. The family is, so to speak, the domestic church. In it parents should, by their word and example, be the first preachers of the faith to their children; they should encourage them in the vocation which is proper to

---

38 Pope Francis, "General Audience," April 2, 2014, no. 3, http://w2.vatican.va/content/francesco/en/audiences/2014/documents/papa-francesco_20140402_udienza-generale.html.

each of them, fostering with special care vocation to a sacred state.[39]

POPE ST. PAUL VI

Educators in Prayer

B y reason of their dignity and mission, Christian parents have the specific responsibility of educating their children in prayer, introducing them to gradual discovery of the mystery of God and to personal dialogue with Him: "It is particularly in the Christian family, enriched by the grace and the office of the sacrament of Matrimony, that from the earliest years children should be taught, according to the faith received in Baptism, to have a knowledge of God, to worship Him and to love their neighbor."

The concrete example and living witness of parents is fundamental and irreplaceable in educating their children to pray. Only by praying together with their children can a father and mother—exercising their royal priesthood—penetrate the innermost depths of their children's hearts and leave an impression that the future events in their lives will not be able to efface. Let us again listen to the appeal made by Paul VI to parents: "Mothers, do you teach your children the Christian prayers? Do

---

39 Pope Saint Paul VI, Dogmatic Constitution *Lumen Gentium* (1964), no. 11.

you prepare them, in conjunction with the priests, for the sacraments that they receive when they are young: Confession, Communion and Confirmation? Do you encourage them when they are sick to think of Christ suffering to invoke the aid of the Blessed Virgin and the saints? Do you say the family rosary together? And you, fathers, do you pray with your children, with the whole domestic community, at least sometimes? Your example of honesty in thought and action, joined to some common prayer, is a lesson for life, an act of worship of singular value. In this way you bring peace to your homes: Pax huic domui. Remember, it is thus that you build up the Church."[40]

POPE ST. JOHN PAUL II

PASTORAL GUIDANCE

Women in the Church and in the World

Among the fundamental values linked to women's actual lives is what has been called a "capacity for the other". Although a certain type of feminist rhetoric makes demands "for ourselves", women preserve the deep intuition of the goodness in their lives of those actions which elicit life,

---

40 Pope Saint John Paul II, *Familiaris Consortio*.

and contribute to the growth and protection of the other. . . .

In this perspective, one understands the irreplaceable role of women in all aspects of family and social life involving human relationships and caring for others. Here what John Paul II has termed the genius of women becomes very clear. It implies first of all that women be significantly and actively present in the family, "the primordial and, in a certain sense sovereign society", since it is here above all that the features of a people take shape; it is here that its members acquire basic teachings. They learn to love inasmuch as they are unconditionally loved, they learn respect for others inasmuch as they are respected, they learn to know the face of God inasmuch as they receive a first revelation of it from a father and a mother full of attention in their regard. Whenever these fundamental experiences are lacking, society as a whole suffers violence and becomes in turn the progenitor of more violence. It means also that women should be present in the world of work and in the organization of society, and that women should have access to positions of responsibility which allow them to inspire the policies of nations and to promote innovative solutions to economic and social problems. . . .

It is from Mary that the Church always learns the intimacy of Christ. Mary, who carried the small child of Bethlehem in her arms, teaches us to recognize the infinite humility of God. She who received the broken body of Jesus from the Cross shows the Church how to receive all those in this world whose lives have been wounded by violence and sin. From Mary, the Church learns the meaning of the power of love, as revealed by God in the life of his beloved Son: "he has scattered the proud in the thoughts of their heart . . . he has lifted up the lowly" (Lk 1:51-52). From Mary, the disciples of Christ continually receive the sense and the delight of praise for the work of God's hands: "The Almighty has done great things for me" (Lk 1:49). They learn that they are in the world to preserve the memory of those "great things", and to keep vigil in expectation of the day of the Lord.[41]

---

41 Congregation for the Doctrine of the Faith, *Letter to the Bishops of the Catholic Church on the Collaboration of Men and Women in the Church and in the World*, May 31, 2004.

8

SCRIPTURES FOR WOMEN

A VARIETY OF VERSES

It Is Not Good That Man Should Be Alone

Then the LORD God said, "It is not good that the man should be alone; I will make him a helper fit for him." So out of the ground the LORD God formed every beast of the field and every bird of the air, and brought them to the man to see what he would call them; and whatever the man called every living creature, that was its name. The man gave names to all cattle, and to the birds of the air, and to every beast of the field; but for the man there was not found a helper fit for him. So the LORD God caused a deep sleep to fall upon the man, and while he slept took one of his ribs and closed up its place with flesh; and the rib which the LORD God had taken from the man he made into a woman and brought her to the man. Then the man said,

"This at last is bone of my bones

and flesh of my flesh;
she shall be called Woman,
because she was taken out of Man."

Therefore a man leaves his father and his mother and cleaves to his wife, and they become one flesh.
Gn 2:18–24

Ode to a Capable Wife

A good wife who can find?
She is far more precious than jewels.
The heart of her husband trusts in her,
and he will have no lack of gain.
She does him good, and not harm,
all the days of her life.
She seeks wool and flax,
and works with willing hands.
She is like the ships of the merchant,
she brings her food from afar.
She rises while it is yet night
and provides food for her household
and tasks for her maidens.
She considers a field and buys it;
with the fruit of her hands she plants a
vineyard.
She girds her loins with strength
and makes her arms strong.
She perceives that her merchandise is
profitable.

Her lamp does not go out at night.
She puts her hands to the distaff,
        and her hands hold the spindle.
She opens her hand to the poor,
        and reaches out her hands to the needy.
She is not afraid of snow for her household,
        for all her household are clothed in
        scarlet.
She makes herself coverings;
        her clothing is fine linen and purple.
Her husband is known in the gates,
        when he sits among the elders of the
        land.
She makes linen garments and sells them;
        she delivers girdles to the merchant.
Strength and dignity are her clothing,
        and she laughs at the time to come.
She opens her mouth with wisdom,
        and the teaching of kindness is on her
        tongue.
She looks well to the ways of her household,
        and does not eat the bread of idleness.
Her children rise up and call her blessed;
        her husband also, and he praises her:
"Many women have done excellently,
        but you surpass them all."
Charm is deceitful, and beauty is vain,
        but a woman who fears the Lord is to be
        praised.
Give her of the fruit of her hands,

and let her works praise her in the gates.
Prv 31:10–31

Jesus Anointed at Bethany

Now when Jesus was at Bethany in the house of Simon the leper, a woman came up to him with an alabaster jar of very expensive ointment, and she poured it on his head, as he sat at table. But when the disciples saw it, they were indignant, saying, "Why this waste? For this ointment might have been sold for a large sum, and given to the poor." But Jesus, aware of this, said to them, "Why do you trouble the woman? For she has done a beautiful thing to me. For you always have the poor with you, but you will not always have me. In pouring this ointment on my body she has done it to prepare me for burial. Truly, I say to you, wherever this gospel is preached in the whole world, what she has done will be told in memory of her." Mt 26:6–13

Jesus Provides for Mary

But standing by the cross of Jesus were his mother, and his mother's sister, Mary the wife of Clopas, and Mary Magdalene. When Jesus saw his mother, and the disciple whom he loved standing near, he said to his mother, "Woman, behold, your son!" Then he said to the disciple,

"Behold, your mother!" And from that hour the disciple took her to his own home. Jn 19:25–27

The Faith of the Samaritan Woman

The woman said to him, "Sir, I perceive that you are a prophet. Our fathers worshiped on this mountain; and you say that in Jerusalem is the place where men ought to worship." Jesus said to her, "Woman, believe me, the hour is coming when neither on this mountain nor in Jerusalem will you worship the Father. You worship what you do not know; we worship what we know, for salvation is from the Jews. But the hour is coming, and now is, when the true worshipers will worship the Father in spirit and truth, for such the Father seeks to worship him. God is spirit, and those who worship him must worship in spirit and truth." The woman said to him, "I know that Messiah is coming (he who is called Christ); when he comes, he will show us all things." Jesus said to her, "I who speak to you am he." Jn 4:19–26

Under Christ, All Are Children of God

There is neither Jew nor Greek, there is neither slave nor free, there is neither male nor female; for you are all one in Christ Jesus. Gal 3:28

The Wedding at Cana

On the third day there was a marriage at Cana in Galilee, and the mother of Jesus was there; Jesus also was invited to the marriage, with his disciples. When the wine failed, the mother of Jesus said to him, "They have no wine." And Jesus said to her, "O woman, what have you to do with me? My hour has not yet come." His mother said to the servants, "Do whatever he tells you." Now six stone jars were standing there, for the Jewish rites of purification, each holding twenty or thirty gallons. Jesus said to them, "Fill the jars with water." And they filled them up to the brim. He said to them, "Now draw some out, and take it to the steward of the feast." So they took it. When the steward of the feast tasted the water now become wine, and did not know where it came from (though the servants who had drawn the water knew), the steward of the feast called the bridegroom and said to him, "Every man serves the good wine first; and when men have drunk freely, then the poor wine; but you have kept the good wine until now." This, the first of his signs, Jesus did at Cana in Galilee, and manifested his glory; and his disciples believed in him. Jn 2:1–11

The Ten Commandments

A nd God spoke all these words, saying,
    "I am the LORD your God, who brought you out of the land of Egypt, out of the house of bondage.

"You shall have no other gods before me.

"You shall not make for yourself a graven image, or any likeness of anything that is in heaven above, or that is in the earth beneath, or that is in the water under the earth; you shall not bow down to them or serve them; for I the LORD your God am a jealous God, visiting the iniquity of the fathers upon the children to the third and the fourth generation of those who hate me, but showing steadfast love to thousands of those who love me and keep my commandments.

"You shall not take the name of the LORD your God in vain; for the LORD will not hold him guiltless who takes his name in vain.

"Remember the sabbath day, to keep it holy. Six days you shall labor, and do all your work; but the seventh day is a sabbath to the LORD your God; in it you shall not do any work, you, or your son, or your daughter, your manservant, or your maidservant, or your cattle, or the sojourner who is within your gates; for in six days the LORD made heaven and earth, the sea, and all that is in them, and rested the seventh day; therefore the LORD blessed the sabbath day and hallowed it.

"Honor your father and your mother, that your days may be long in the land which the LORD your God gives you.

"You shall not kill.

"You shall not commit adultery.

"You shall not steal.

"You shall not bear false witness against your neighbor.

"You shall not covet your neighbor's house; you shall not covet your neighbor's wife, or his manservant, or his maidservant, or his ox, or his ass, or anything that is your neighbor's." Ex 20:1–17

There are six things which the LORD hates,
        seven which are an abomination to him:
haughty eyes, a lying tongue,
        and hands that shed innocent blood,
a heart that devises wicked plans,
        feet that make haste to run to evil,
a false witness who breathes out lies,
        and a man who sows discord among
        brothers. Prv 6:16–19

Ruth's Beautiful Devotion to Her Mother-in-Law

In the days when the judges ruled there was a famine in the land, and a certain man of Bethlehem in Judah went to sojourn in the country of

Moab, he and his wife and his two sons. The name of the man was Elimelech and the name of his wife Naomi, and the names of his two sons were Mahlon and Chilion; they were Ephrathites from Bethlehem in Judah. They went into the country of Moab and remained there. But Elimelech, the husband of Naomi, died, and she was left with her two sons. These took Moabite wives; the name of the one was Orpah and the name of the other Ruth. They lived there about ten years; and both Mahlon and Chilion died, so that the woman was bereft of her two sons and her husband.

. . . But Naomi said to her two daughters-in-law, "Go, return each of you to her mother's house. May the LORD deal kindly with you, as you have dealt with the dead and with me." . . . And they said to her, "No, we will return with you to your people." . . . "Would you therefore refrain from marrying? No, my daughters, for it is exceedingly bitter to me for your sake that the hand of the LORD has gone forth against me." Then they lifted up their voices and wept again; and Orpah kissed her mother-in-law, but Ruth clung to her.

And she said, "See, your sister-in-law has gone back to her people and to her gods; return after your sister-in-law." But Ruth said, "Entreat me not to leave you or to return from following you; for where you go I will go, and where you lodge I will lodge; your people shall be my people, and your God my God; where you die I will die, and there will I be buried. May the LORD do so to me and more also if even death parts me from you." And when Naomi saw that she was determined to go with her, she said no more. Ru 1:1–5, 8, 10, 13–18

VERSES OF RECEPTIVITY

The virgin's name was Mary. And he came to her and said, "Hail, full of grace, the Lord is with you!" But she was greatly troubled at the saying, and considered in her mind what sort of greeting this might be. And the angel said to her, "Do not be afraid, Mary, for you have found favor with God. And behold, you will conceive in your womb and bear a son, and you shall call his name Jesus.

He will be great, and will be called the Son of
    the Most High;
and the Lord God will give to him the throne of
    his father David,
and he will reign over the house of Jacob for
    ever;
and of his kingdom there will be no end."

And Mary said to the angel, "How can this be, since I have no husband?" And the angel said to her,

"The Holy Spirit will come upon you,

and the power of the Most High will
    overshadow you;
therefore the child to be born will be called
    holy,
the Son of God.

And behold, your kinswoman Elizabeth in her old age has also conceived a son; and this is the sixth month with her who was called barren. For with God nothing will be impossible." And Mary said, "Behold, I am the handmaid of the Lord; let it be to me according to your word." And the angel departed from her. Lk 1:27–38

VERSES OF SENSITIVITY

On the third day there was a marriage at Cana in Galilee, and the mother of Jesus was there; Jesus also was invited to the marriage, with his disciples. When the wine failed, the mother of Jesus said to him, "They have no wine." And Jesus said to her, "O woman, what have you to do with me? My hour has not yet come." His mother said to the servants, "Do whatever he tells you." Now six stone jars were standing there, for the Jewish rites of purification, each holding twenty or thirty gallons. Jesus said to them, "Fill the jars with water." And they filled them up to the brim. Jn 2:1–7

The Spirit of the Lord GOD is upon me,
　　　　because the LORD has anointed me
to bring good tidings to the afflicted;
　　　　he has sent me to bind up the
　　　　brokenhearted,
to proclaim liberty to the captives,
　　　　and the opening of the prison to those
　　　　who are bound. Is 61:1

———

If one member suffers, all suffer together; if one
member is honored, all rejoice together. 1 Cor 12:26

VERSES OF COMPASSION

Put on then, as God's chosen ones, holy and
beloved, compassion, kindness, lowliness,
meekness, and patience, forbearing one another
and, if one has a complaint against another, forgiving each other; as the Lord has forgiven you,
so you also must forgive. And above all these put
on love, which binds everything together in perfect harmony. And let the peace of Christ rule in
your hearts, to which indeed you were called in the
one body. And be thankful. Let the word of Christ
dwell in you richly, as you teach and admonish one
another in all wisdom, and as you sing psalms and
hymns and spiritual songs with thankfulness in
your hearts to God. And whatever you do, in word

or deed, do everything in the name of the Lord
Jesus, giving thanks to God the Father through him.
Col 3:12–17

And the LORD said to Moses, "This very thing
that you have spoken I will do; for you have found
favor in my sight, and I know you by name." Moses
said, "I pray thee, show me thy glory." And he said,
"I will make all my goodness pass before you, and
will proclaim before you my name 'The LORD'; and
I will be gracious to whom I will be gracious, and
will show mercy on whom I will show mercy." Ex
33:17–19

Therefore the LORD waits to be gracious to you;
    therefore he exalts himself to show
    mercy to you.
For the LORD is a God of justice;
    blessed are all those who wait for him.

Yea, O people in Zion who dwell at Jerusalem;
you shall weep no more. He will surely be gracious
to you at the sound of your cry; when he hears it,
he will answer you. And though the LORD give you
the bread of adversity and the water of affliction, yet
your Teacher will not hide himself any more, but
your eyes shall see your Teacher. And your ears shall

hear a word behind you, saying, "This is the way,
walk in it." Is 30:18–21

Thus says the LORD:
"In a time of favor I have answered you,
        in a day of salvation I have helped you;
I have kept you and given you
        as a covenant to the people,
to establish the land,
        to apportion the desolate heritages;
saying to the prisoners, 'Come forth,'
        to those who are in darkness, 'Appear.'
They shall feed along the ways,
        on all bare heights shall be their pasture;
they shall not hunger or thirst,
        neither scorching wind nor sun shall
        smite them,
for he who has pity on them will lead them,
        and by springs of water will guide them.
And I will make all my mountains a way,
        and my highways shall be raised up." Is
    49:8–11

Can a woman forget her sucking child,
        that she should have no compassion on
        the son of her womb?
Even these may forget,
        yet I will not forget you.

Behold, I have graven you on the palms of my hands;
> your walls are continually before me. Is
> 49:15–16

———

For this is like the days of Noah to me:
> as I swore that the waters of Noah
> should no more go over the earth,
so I have sworn that I will not be angry with you
> and will not rebuke you.
For the mountains may depart
> and the hills be removed,
but my steadfast love shall not depart from you,
> and my covenant of peace shall not be
> removed,
> says the LORD, who has compassion on
> you. Is 54:9–10

———

Be patient, therefore, brethren, until the coming of the Lord. Behold, the farmer waits for the precious fruit of the earth, being patient over it until it receives the early and the late rain. You also be patient. Establish your hearts, for the coming of the Lord is at hand. Do not grumble, brethren, against one another, that you may not be judged; behold, the Judge is standing at the doors. As an example of suffering and patience, brethren, take the prophets who spoke in the name of the Lord. Behold, we call those happy who were steadfast. You have heard of the steadfastness of Job, and you have seen the purpose of the Lord, how the Lord is compassionate and merciful. Jas 5:7–11

The LORD is good to those who wait for him,
     to the soul that seeks him.
It is good that one should wait quietly
     for the salvation of the LORD.
It is good for a man that he bear
     the yoke in his youth.
Let him sit alone in silence
     when he has laid it on him;
let him put his mouth in the dust—
     there may yet be hope;
let him give his cheek to the smiter,
     and be filled with insults.
For the Lord will not
     cast off for ever,
but, though he cause grief, he will have
     compassion
        according to the abundance of his
        steadfast love;
for he does not willingly afflict
     or grieve the sons of men. Lam 3:25–33

Have mercy on me, O God, according to your
     steadfast love;

according to your abundant mercy blot out my
transgressions. Ps 51:1

Gracious is the LORD, and righteous;
    our God is merciful.
The LORD preserves the simple;
    when I was brought low, he saved me.
Return, O my soul, to your rest;
    for the LORD has dealt bountifully with
    you. Ps 116:5–7

The LORD is gracious and merciful,
    slow to anger and abounding in
    steadfast love.
The LORD is good to all,
    and his compassion is over all that he
    has made. Ps 145:8–9

Blessed be the God and Father of our Lord Jesus
Christ, the Father of mercies and God of all comfort, who comforts us in all our affliction, so that
we may be able to comfort those who are in any
affliction, with the comfort with which we ourselves are comforted by God. For as we share abundantly in Christ's sufferings, so through Christ we
share abundantly in comfort too. If we are afflicted,
it is for your comfort and salvation; and if we are

comforted, it is for your comfort, which you experience when you patiently endure the same sufferings
that we suffer. Our hope for you is unshaken; for we
know that as you share in our sufferings, you will
also share in our comfort. 2 Cor 1:3–7

So if there is any encouragement in Christ, any
incentive of love, any participation in the Spirit, any
affection and sympathy, complete my joy by being
of the same mind, having the same love, being in
full accord and of one mind. Do nothing from selfishness or conceit, but in humility count others better than yourselves. Phil 2:1–3

And Jesus went about all the cities and villages,
teaching in their synagogues and preaching the gospel of the kingdom, and healing every disease and
every infirmity. When he saw the crowds, he had
compassion for them, because they were harassed
and helpless, like sheep without a shepherd. Then
he said to his disciples, "The harvest is plentiful,
but the laborers are few; pray therefore the Lord of
the harvest to send out laborers into his harvest."
Mt 9:35–38

And as they went out of Jericho, a great crowd
followed him. And behold, two blind men sitting

by the roadside, when they heard that Jesus was passing by, cried out, "Have mercy on us, Son of David!" The crowd rebuked them, telling them to be silent; but they cried out the more, "Lord, have mercy on us, Son of David!" And Jesus stopped and called them, saying, "What do you want me to do for you?" They said to him, "Lord, let our eyes be opened." And Jesus in pity touched their eyes, and immediately they received their sight and followed him. Mt 20:29–34

Let all bitterness and wrath and anger and clamor and slander be put away from you, with all malice, and be kind to one another, tenderhearted, forgiving one another, as God in Christ forgave you. Eph 4:31–32

Rejoice with those who rejoice, weep with those who weep. Rom 12:15

I will arise and go to my father, and I will say to him, "Father, I have sinned against heaven and before you; I am no longer worthy to be called your son; treat me as one of your hired servants."' And he arose and came to his father. But while he was yet at a distance, his father saw him and had compassion, and ran and embraced him and kissed him. Lk 15:18–20

But a Samaritan, as he journeyed, came to where he was; and when he saw him, he had compassion, and went to him and bound up his wounds, pouring on oil and wine; then he set him on his own beast and brought him to an inn, and took care of him. And the next day he took out two denarii and gave them to the innkeeper, saying, "Take care of him; and whatever more you spend, I will repay you when I come back." Lk 10:33–35

VERSES OF GENEROSITY

One man gives freely, yet grows all the
   richer;
     another withholds what he should give,
     and only suffers want.
A liberal man will be enriched,
     and one who waters will himself be
     watered. Prv 11:24–25

He who sows sparingly will also reap sparingly, and he who sows bountifully will also reap bountifully. Each one must do as he has made up his mind, not reluctantly or under compulsion, for God loves

SCRIPTURES FOR WOMEN 127

a cheerful giver. And God is able to provide you with every blessing in abundance, so that you may always have enough of everything and may provide in abundance for every good work. 2 Cor 9:6–8

For if the readiness is there, it is acceptable according to what a man has, not according to what he has not. 2 Cor 8:12

It is well with the man who deals generously
    and lends,
        who conducts his affairs with justice. Ps
    112:5

To him who strikes you on the cheek, offer the other also; and from him who takes away your cloak do not withhold your coat as well. Give to every one who begs from you; and of him who takes away your goods do not ask them again. Lk 6:29–30

In all things I have shown you that by so toiling one must help the weak, remembering the words of the Lord Jesus, how he said, "It is more blessed to give than to receive." Acts 20:35

If any of you lacks wisdom, let him ask God, who gives to all men generously and without reproaching, and it will be given him. *Jas 1:5*

Let brotherly love continue. Do not neglect to show hospitality to strangers, for thereby some have entertained angels unawares. Remember those who are in prison, as though in prison with them. *Heb 13:1–3*

But if any one has the world's goods and sees his brother in need, yet closes his heart against him, how does God's love abide in him? *1 Jn 3:17*

VERSES OF BEAUTY

Charm is deceitful, and beauty is vain, but a woman who fears the Lord is to be praised. *Prv 31:30*

Let not yours be the outward adorning with braiding of hair, decoration of gold, and wearing of robes, but let it be the hidden person of the heart with the imperishable jewel of a gentle and quiet spirit, which in God's sight is very precious. *1 Pt 3:3–4*

Finally, brethren, whatever is true, whatever is honorable, whatever is just, whatever is pure, whatever is lovely, whatever is gracious, if there is any excellence, if there is anything worthy of praise, think about these things. Phil 4:8

———

Until the day breathes
    and the shadows flee,
I will hie me to the mountain of myrrh
    and the hill of frankincense.
You are all fair, my love;
    there is no flaw in you.
Come with me from Lebanon, my bride;
    come with me from Lebanon. Sg 4:6–8

———

Do not look on his appearance or on the height of his stature, because I have rejected him; for the LORD sees not as man sees; man looks on the outward appearance, but the Lord looks on the heart. 1 Sm 16:7

———

A gracious woman gets honor. Prv 11:16

———

A man is known by his appearance,
    and a sensible man is known by his face,
when you meet him.

A man's attire and open-mouthed laughter,
    and a man's manner of walking, show
  what he is. Sir 19:29–30

Your heart was proud because of your beauty;
    you corrupted your wisdom for the sake
  of your splendor. Ez 28:17

How graceful are your feet in sandals,
    O queenly maiden!
Your rounded thighs are like jewels,
    the work of a master hand. Sg 7:1

VERSES OF CHILDREN

Hear, O Israel: The LORD our God is one LORD; and you shall love the LORD your God with all your heart, and with all your soul, and with all your might. And these words which I command you this day shall be upon your heart; and you shall teach them diligently to your children, and shall talk of them when you sit in your house, and when you walk by the way, and when you lie down, and when you rise. Dt 6:4–7

Keep his statutes and his commandments, which I command you this day, that it may go well with you, and with your children after you, and that you may prolong your days in the land which the LORD your God gives you for ever. Dt 4:40

———

O LORD, our Lord,
how majestic is thy name in all the earth!
Thou whose glory above the heavens is chanted
        by the mouth of babes and infants,
thou hast founded a bulwark because of thy foes,
        to still the enemy and the avenger. Ps 8:1–2

———

Lo, sons are a heritage from the LORD,
        the fruit of the womb a reward.
Like arrows in the hand of a warrior
        are the sons of one's youth.
Happy is the man who has
        his quiver full of them!
He shall not be put to shame
        when he speaks with his enemies in the
        gate. Ps 127:3–5

———

Grandchildren are the crown of the aged,
        and the glory of sons is their fathers. Prv
        17:6

He who spares the rod hates his son,
　　　but he who loves him is diligent to
　　　discipline him. Prv 13:24

But as for you, continue in what you have learned
and have firmly believed, knowing from whom you
learned it and how from childhood you have been
acquainted with the sacred writings which are able
to instruct you for salvation through faith in Christ
Jesus. 2 Tm 3:14–15

And calling to him a child, he put him in the
midst of them, and said, "Truly, I say to you, unless
you turn and become like children, you will never
enter the kingdom of heaven. Whoever humbles
himself like this child, he is the greatest in the kingdom of heaven.

"Whoever receives one such child in my name
receives me; but whoever causes one of these little
ones who believe in me to sin, it would be better for
him to have a great millstone fastened round his
neck and to be drowned in the depth of the sea."
Mt 18:2–6

When a woman is in travail she has sorrow,
because her hour has come; but when she is delivered of the child, she no longer remembers the

anguish, for joy that a child is born into the world. Jn 16:21

———

And they were bringing children to him, that he might touch them; and the disciples rebuked them. But when Jesus saw it he was indignant, and said to them, "Let the children come to me, do not hinder them; for to such belongs the kingdom of God. Truly, I say to you, whoever does not receive the kingdom of God like a child shall not enter it." And he took them in his arms and blessed them, laying his hands upon them. Mk 10:13–16

———

No greater joy can I have than this, to hear that my children follow the truth. 3 Jn 4

———

See that you do not despise one of these little ones; for I tell you that in heaven their angels always behold the face of my Father who is in heaven. Mt 18:10

———

Train up a child in the way he should go,
     and when he is old he will not depart
     from it. Prv 22:6

Who is like the LORD our God,
      who is seated on high,
who looks far down
      upon the heavens and the earth?
He raises the poor from the dust,
      and lifts the needy from the ash heap,
to make them sit with princes,
      with the princes of his people.
He gives the barren woman a home,
      making her the joyous mother of
      children.
Praise the LORD! Ps 113:5–9

———

For you formed my inward parts,
      you knitted me together in my mother's
      womb.
I praise thee, for thou art fearful and wonderful.
      Wonderful are your works!
You know me right well;
      my frame was not hidden from you,
when I was being made in secret,
      intricately wrought in the depths of the
      earth.
Your eyes beheld my unformed substance;
      in your book were written, every one of
      them,
the days that were formed for me,
      when as yet there was none of them. Ps
      139:13–16

Children, obey your parents in the Lord, for this is right. "Honor your father and mother" (this is the first commandment with a promise), "that it may be well with you and that you may live long on the earth." Eph 6:1–3

VERSES ABOUT WORRY

Unless the LORD builds the house,
     those who build it labor in vain.
Unless the LORD watches over the city,
     the watchman stays awake in vain.
It is in vain that you rise up early and go late to
     rest,
eating the bread of anxious toil;
     for he gives to his beloved sleep. Ps
127:1–2

Have no anxiety about anything, but in everything by prayer and supplication with thanksgiving let your requests be made known to God. And the peace of God, which passes all understanding, will keep your hearts and your minds in Christ Jesus.

Finally, brethren, whatever is true, whatever is honorable, whatever is just, whatever is pure, whatever is lovely, whatever is gracious, if there is any excellence, if there is anything worthy of praise, think about these things. What you have learned and received and heard and seen in me, do; and the God of peace will be with you. Phil 4:6–9

And he said to his disciples, "Therefore I tell you, do not be anxious about your life, what you shall eat, nor about your body, what you shall put on. For life is more than food, and the body more than clothing. Consider the ravens: they neither sow nor reap, they have neither storehouse nor barn, and yet God feeds them. Of how much more value are you than the birds! And which of you by being anxious can add a cubit to his span of life? If then you are not able to do as small a thing as that, why are you anxious about the rest? Consider the lilies, how they grow; they neither toil nor spin; yet I tell you, even Solomon in all his glory was not arrayed like one of these. But if God so clothes the grass which is alive in the field today and tomorrow is thrown into the oven, how much more will he clothe you, O men of little faith!" Lk 12:22–28

Therefore I tell you, do not be anxious about your life, what you shall eat or what you shall drink, nor about your body, what you shall put on. Is not life more than food, and the body more than clothing? Look at the birds of the air: they neither sow nor reap nor gather into barns, and yet your heavenly Father feeds them. Are you not of more value than they? And which of you by being anxious can add one cubit to his span of life? Mt 6:25–27

———

Come to me, all who labor and are heavy laden, and I will give you rest. Take my yoke upon you, and learn from me; for I am gentle and lowly in heart, and you will find rest for your souls. For my yoke is easy, and my burden is light. Mt 11:28–30

———

Peace I leave with you; my peace I give to you; not as the world gives do I give to you. Let not your hearts be troubled, neither let them be afraid. Jn 14:27

———

Cast all your anxiety on him, for he cares about you. 1 Pt 5:7

———

Anxiety in a man's heart weighs him down,
      but a good word makes him glad. Prv 12:25

———

But now thus says the LORD,
he who created you, O Jacob,
      he who formed you, O Israel:
"Fear not, for I have redeemed you;
      I have called you by name, you are mine.

When you pass through the waters I will be with
    you;
    and through the rivers, they shall not
    overwhelm you;
when you walk through fire you shall not be
    burned,
    and the flame shall not consume you.
For I am the LORD your God,
    the Holy One of Israel, your Savior. Is 43:1–3

What then shall we say to this? If God is for us,
who is against us? Rom 8:31

9

THE SAINTS AND OTHER EXEMPLARS

LIVES OF THE SAINTS

St. Anne, Mother of the Blessed Virgin

St. Anne, the mother of the Blessed Virgin, was a native of Bethlehem, a city two miles distant from Jerusalem and frequently mentioned in Scripture. Having passed her youth in unstained purity, she was married to a man named Joachim, who was born at Nazareth in Galilee. They lived in such love and harmony, and at the same time so piously, that one could justly say of them what St. Luke writes of Zachary and Elizabeth: "Both of them were righteous before God, living blamelessly according to all the commandments and regulations of the Lord" (Lk 1:6). They divided their income into three parts, the first of which was used for the honor of God and to adorn the Temple, the second to assist the poor, and the third for their own subsistence. They employed the day in prayer, work suitable to their station in life, and charitable deeds.

Their only grief was that, although long-married, they had no children; and an infertile marriage was at that time considered a disgrace—almost a sign of a divine curse. Saddened by this, Sts. Anne and Joachim prayed with many tears that God would take pity on them and remove the sorrow that was weighing them down. But when, after having prayed long and earnestly they were not heard, they determined to bear patiently the will of the Almighty. Since St. Anne knew that God asked continual prayer, and that he had not given to his people a certain time to ask for grace, she never ceased to implore heaven with confidence, for everything she believed was for his honor and her own salvation. One day in the Temple, she felt her distress so deeply that she wept bitterly, but she remembered, at the same time, that there had been another Anne, spouse of Elcana, who had been afflicted as she was. God at last had answered her prayers, making her the mother of the great prophet Samuel. While thinking of this, she perceived in herself an invincible desire to beg the Lord for a similar grace. Hence, she repeated her prayer with earnest fervor, promising at the same time, that if God would grant her a child, she would consecrate the child in the Temple to his divine service, just as the mother of Samuel had done.

According to the opinion of the Holy Fathers, God answered the trusting prayer of his servant.

He sent an angel, who announced to Anne that she would give birth to a daughter who would be blessed among women. It is also believed that the angel told St. Anne the name which she should give to the blessed fruit of her womb. The same revelation was made to St. Joachim, and the happiness of both and their gratitude to the Almighty can be easily imagined. Their happiness was crowned when St. Anne gave birth to Mary, who was elected by God from all eternity to become the mother of his only Son. The blessed child was wise beyond her years, and her whole being so angelically innocent that her education was an easy task. St. Anne deemed herself the happiest mother in the world, because God had entrusted to her so priceless a child. Who can doubt that St. Anne, who was the mother of the Blessed Virgin, was given extraordinary graces? St. Anne did not fail to return to God what she had received from him and to offer willingly what she had so willingly promised. Hardly had Mary reached the age of three when Anne and Joachim presented her to the priest of the temple at Jerusalem and consecrated her through him to the Almighty. Thus, Mary was received among the number of those who, under the direction of the priests, served God in the Temple, and were led in the path of virtue. After they had piously offered this agreeable sacrifice, the parents of the Blessed Virgin returned home, and spent the remainder of their days in good works, which were

continued by St. Anne, when she became a widow
by the death of her holy spouse.

As Anne had been an example to the virgins
before her marriage, as well as a perfect model of a
wife, so she was a shining light in her widowhood,
a shining light, possessing all those qualities which
St. Paul afterwards required of a Christian widow,
in his first letter to Timothy (1 Tm 5). She went frequently to Jerusalem to see her holy daughter, and
died, according to several authors, in the seventy-
ninth year of her age. Mary, who at that time still
lived in the temple, closed her eyes.

As one cannot give to the Blessed Virgin a higher
title than to call her Mother of God, thus St. Anne
cannot be more exalted than when she is called
the mother of she who bore the Son of God. And
for the very reason that she was chosen to be her
mother, we must believe that the Almighty favored
her here upon earth, with grace above all the saints,
and raised her to high glory in heaven. Hence, we
may rightly suppose, that her intercession with
God is most powerful, and this is testified by many
examples.

Practical Considerations

S aint Anne truly offers many examples for living a holy life. When St. Anne realized that,
despite many prayers, God sent her no children, she
submitted to his divine will and bore her trial with

patience. This is how Christians should act when God denies their prayers because all he does is the best for them. He has his reasons for acting as he does, and his reasons are always just even when they are hard to understand. When St. Anne received from God what she had so constantly prayed for during many years, she gave thanks to him, educated her daughter piously, and early consecrated Mary to the service of heaven. Thus, should all Christian parents act. Their greatest care should be to teach their children early to serve God and bring them up for heaven. If one of their children has a calling for a religious life, they must not oppose it. St. Anne deprived herself of the great comfort which her daughter's presence gave her, when for the love of God, she consecrated her, by the hands of the priest, to the service of our Lord. Shouldn't Christian parents do the same and willingly consecrate their child to God, to whom he or she belongs much more than to themselves?

St. Anne prayed long yet without complaint against God. She continued her prayers with undiminished confidence until she at last received what she had asked. God has many reasons for not always hearing our prayers immediately, but are we praying as well as we can? Sometimes we pray when we are not in a state of grace; or we live in sin without repenting, or without the intention of bettering our life. In such cases, perhaps our prayers are less sincere. Sometimes we pray without devotion and reverence. At another time, we pray only for things which God knows to be hurtful to us, although we may imagine that they are for our good. In such cases, God bestows a grace upon us by not hearing us. Also, there are times when we are deaf when God called to us; how can we ask that he should directly hear us? "What right have we," asks St. Salvianus, "to complain, when God does not hear us, or, so to speak, seems to neglect our prayers when we have so often not listened to Him, and so frequently despised His laws? What is more just than that He should not listen to us, because we heard not Him, and that He should neglect our prayers, as we did His laws?" We are blessed indeed that our Father is so generous and forgiving. Further, God does not always hear us immediately, in order that we may pray more fervently and esteem so much more highly the favors he bestows. He does it also to try our patience and our trust in his mercy, or that we may be more deserving of his grace by continual prayers. Finally, he may do it to give us something better than we asked for.

When all this is considered, can we complain when the Almighty doesn't answer our prayers immediately? Continue in them. Persist. Perform them in the right spirit and you will experience the truth of the words of St. Bernard: "God either gives us what we ask, or something else, which is more helpful to us."

St. Martha

St. Martha, more than once mentioned in the Gospel, was born of illustrious parents. Her father was of Syria, her mother of Judaea, and after their death, she inherited their house and estate at Bethany. She exercised herself freely in good works, especially in those of charity, and was one of the first women who, by attending the instructions of Christ, and by his miracles, recognized in him the true Messiah. From that hour her heart was filled with the most devoted love to the Lord, who, according to the Gospel, returned her pious affection. The conversion of her sister Magdalen was in a great measure her work, as she persuaded her to hear Christ's sermons. After Magdalen's conversion, she and Martha accompanied Christ from place to place, desiring not to lose any of his divine instructions. Frequently had Martha the grace to receive our Lord into her house and to see him sitting at her table. One day, being so honored, she prepared, with her own hands, everything that she would set before our Savior, anxious that he should be served well. Seeing that her sister Magdalen meanwhile sat quietly at the feet of Christ, without assisting her, she, mildly complaining, said to the Savior: "Lord, have you no care that my sister has left me alone to serve? Speak to her, therefore, so that she will help me." Christ reproached her somewhat for her too great solicitude for temporal things, with these words, fraught with deep meaning: "Martha, Martha; you are careful and are troubled about many things, but one thing is necessary. Mary has chosen the best part, which shall not be taken away from her." Martha humbly received this kind reproof, this wholesome lesson, and when Christ was at table with Lazarus and Magdalen, she served him, thinking rightly that this was the greatest honor that could be bestowed upon her. Shortly before the Passion of the Savior, Lazarus, her brother, became dangerously sick. She immediately sent a messenger to Christ to announce this to him, in the following words: "He whom you love is sick." Both sisters thought this would be enough to induce Christ to come and heal him. But, as our Lord desired, by raising Lazarus from the dead, to give a still greater proof of his power, he came not until Lazarus was buried. Martha went to meet him when she heard of his arrival, and said: "Lord, if You had been here, my brother had not died. But now, also, I know that whatever you will ask of God, he will give it to You." Christ said to her: "Your brother shall rise again." Martha replied, "I know that he shall rise again in the resurrection at the last day." But Christ said, "I am the resurrection and the life. Whoever believes in me, although he be dead, shall live; and everyone who lives and believes in me, shall not die forever. Do you believe this?" She answered: "Yes, Lord, I believe that you are Christ, the Son of the living God, who have come into the world." When she had said this, she entered her house and announced to her sister the arrival of Christ. Rising hastily, Mary went with her to him. Our Savior, deeply moved by the tears and prayers of the two sisters, called Lazarus again to life, who had been in his grave four days. The joy of Martha and Magdalen was beyond measure and the expression of their gratitude both touching and humble. Nothing more is said of Martha in the Gospel, but it is not doubted that she was, with the other pious women, on Mount Calvary at the time of the Savior's passion, and later also present at his ascension, and the coming of the Holy Spirit.

Practical Considerations

You would think that St. Martha was greatly blessed because she had the high honor to receive our Lord into her house and to serve him. But perhaps ours is a greater happiness? Who is it, whom we receive in Holy Communion, in a much more excellent manner, than Martha received him? Is he not the same Jesus who went into her house? He comes more frequently to you—or is ready to do so—than he visited even Martha. Let's recognize this great blessing and use it to our salvation. May we prepare ourselves to receive our Lord worthily and to serve him well in order that He may one day receive us into His kingdom. To receive Holy Communion is one of the most powerful means to gain salvation. "He that eats this bread shall live forever," says Christ in the Gospel of John. May we live, now, then, in sanctifying grace, and live in heaven, in the presence of the Almighty!

In receiving the Lord into her home, St. Martha seems to have misunderstood something about serving Christ. Why do you think Christ corrects her, although gently, it seems? Martha is troubled over many things, but perhaps not the most necessary thing. What is that thing?

St. Hedwig, Widow

We find an example of all virtues worthy to be imitated in the life of St. Hedwig. St. Hedwig was a woman of noble birth. Already in Hedwig's childhood it was visible that God had given her a mind far beyond her age. She possessed an innate inclination to all virtues, and nothing of what usually delights the young touched her heart. In later years she showed little interest in the honors, riches, and amusements of the world. Reading and praying were her only enjoyments. All her books were devout works, and her prayers were said mostly before an image of the Blessed Virgin, whom she loved and honored like a mother.

When scarcely twelve years old, St. Hedwig was given in marriage to Henry, Duke of Poland and Silesia. Although married so early in life, her conduct was so sensible and virtuous that everyone was greatly astonished at it. Among her maxims was this: "The greater one is by birth, the greater one must be in virtue, and the more distinguished we are in station, the more we must distinguish ourselves by our conduct, in order to be a bright example to others." She became the mother of three sons and three daughters, all of whom she educated most piously. She was a little over twenty, and her husband thirty years of age, when their sixth child was born; after which, desiring to serve God more perfectly, she made a vow before the bishop, in which her husband joined, to live in future in perpetual continence.

From that hour, St. Hedwig grew daily more and more perfect in all Christian virtues, occupying every moment left her from the cares she bestowed upon her children, in prayers and deeds of charity. She found great comfort in assisting at Holy Mass; hence, she was not satisfied with one, but went to as many as she could; and the way she conducted herself in church revealed her deep devotion. Towards widows and orphans, her kindness was truly motherly, and many of them she fed in her palace, serving them herself, sometimes on bended knees. She frequently visited the sick in the hospitals, encouraged and comforted them, and assisted all through generous alms. She never hesitated to wash the feet of the lepers, nor to tend the sores of the sufferers. She persuaded the Duke, her husband, to build a large convent not far from Breslau, for the

Cistercian nuns, which she made a home for poor children, who were educated there, and afterwards provided for according to their station. Nothing could be more modest and plainer than the garments of the holy Duchess, and her example in this respect induced others living at court to attire themselves with great simplicity. Amid the dissipation of the court, the saint lived so austere a life that it was more to be admired than to be followed.

To prove her virtue, God visited her with a great many cares and sorrows. The enemy invaded the dominions of her spouse, who was wounded in a battle and made prisoner. When this news was brought to her, she raised her eyes confidently to heaven, saying: "I hope to see him again soon, well and free." She herself went to the Duke who had made her husband prisoner; she spoke so earnestly to him that he granted her husband his liberty. Soon after, her husband became dangerously sick. Hedwig nursed him most faithfully and did everything to make his death happy. To those who pitied her after his death, she said: "We must adore the decrees of the Almighty, not only in days of happiness, but also in those of sorrow and bereavement." Three years later, she lost her firstborn son, who was killed in a battle with the Tartars; and this sad event found her as submissive to the will of Providence as she had been on the death of her husband. Soon after the burial of the Duke, the saint had gone into the convent to be further removed from all temporal vanity, and to serve the Lord more peacefully and perfectly. She observed the regulations of the Order strictly, desiring to do the lowest work and to be considered the least of the sisters. In her austerity toward herself she had now full liberty to satisfy herself. She fasted daily, except on Sundays and festivals; but her fasts were much more rigorous than those of others; for she abstained from all meat and wine, and partook only of herbs, bread and water. She wore, day and night, rough hair-cloth and the iron girdle which she had already worn while at court. She went barefooted over snow and ice, and slept, when well, on the bare boards, and when sick, on straw covered with a coarse cloth. Her sleep lasted hardly three hours before Matins; the remainder of the night she occupied in prayer, which she only interrupted to scourge herself to blood. So severe a life emaciated her body to a skeleton. While working, she always raised her soul to the Most High by mental prayer, and she was often found in an ecstasy, or raised high above the ground. Her conversation was only of God, virtue and piety. Towards the crucified Savior, she bore the deepest devotion, and the mysteries of his bitter passion and death were the objects of her daily meditations, during which she frequently shed tears. Mary, the Blessed Virgin, was most ardently loved by her, and her whole countenance glowed at the bare mention of her name. So holy a life could only be followed by a happy death, of which a severe sickness was the messenger. Before others became aware that her life was in danger, the saint asked for the last Sacraments, and she received them with a devotion which drew tears from the eyes of all who were present.

Before her end, St. Catherine, St. Thecla, St. Ursula, and St. Magdalen appeared to her, all of whom she had greatly honored during her life. These heavenly visitors comforted her and accompanied her to the mansions of everlasting bliss. Twenty-five years after her death, her holy body was exhumed, as so many extraordinary miracles had taken place. On opening the coffin, the whole church was filled with fragrance. The flesh of the whole body was consumed, except that of three fingers on her left hand. With these she had frequently held a picture of the Blessed Virgin, which she constantly carried with her. While dying, she held this picture so fast that after her death it could not be removed, and it was buried with her. Pope Clement IV placed the Duchess among the saints because of her many great virtues, of the miracles which she had wrought while she lived, and of those which took place after her death, through her intercession. The inhabitants of Poland venerate her as one of their special Patrons.

Practical Considerations

"We must adore the decrees of the Almighty not only in happy days, but also in those of sorrow and bereavement," said St. Hedwig, when God deprived her of her beloved spouse, by an early death. She was equally obedient to God's will when she lost her first-born son. How do you act in similar painful circumstances? You will never possess peace of mind, if you do not submit to the will of the Lord. And why shouldn't you do this? The decrees of God are just, although they are hard—often impossible—to understand. Yet nothing that happens to you is unknown to God, and all things that happen to you happen in accordance with his wisdom. All that God permits or ordains, is intended for your welfare. Our faith teaches us this.

It is impossible to avoid the will of God, anyway. There remains nothing to do but to make a virtue of necessity, to accept Providence with a spirit of humility, to submit to it willingly, and to unite your will with that of God. With perseverance you will be calm and contented in all adversities of life, and, at the same time, you will gather merit in heaven. "Make of necessity a virtue," writes St. James of Nisibis, "and as you cannot escape the hand of the Almighty, but must submit to so great a Lord, humble yourself voluntarily under His overwhelming power."

Honor, riches, and the gifts of this world, were no objects of desire to holy St. Hedwig. She sought only heavenly joys. To obtain these, she practiced constant charity to the poor and lived an austere life. Consider that the worldly honors, riches and pleasures she might have enjoyed would long since have passed; the heavenly ones might well have been lost to her. Let us take care that not to become too attached to what is worldly and perishable, but try, through the practice of good works, to obtain that which is eternal. Remember the words of St. Augustine: "No fortune can be considered real fortune, but that which is eternal; no evil can be thought real evil, but that which never ends." If you desire real fortune, honors and joys, strive to obtain those which last for evermore, and be always trying to escape those evils which never end. It is to this end that St. Gregory admonishes us when he says: "At the last day of our life, where will be all that we now seek with so much care, and which we gather so diligently? Therefore, let us not strive after such honors and possessions as we must so soon leave, but let us seek such as we shall have forever. And among, the evils we fear, let us fear and avoid those which the wicked suffer for all eternity."[42]

---

42 Freely adapted from Franz X. Weninger, *Lives of the Saints: Compiled from Authentic Sources with a Practical Instruction on the Life of Each Saint, for Every Day in the Year,* vol. 2, 3 vols. (New York: P. O'Shea, 1876).

St. Clare, Virgin and Abbess

St. Clare, foundress of the Order which bears her name, was born of rich and pious parents, at Assisi, in the district of Umbria, in Italy. She received the name of Clare, which means clear or bright, for the following reason. While her mother, Hortulana, was kneeling before a crucifix, praying that God might aid her in her hour of delivery, she heard the words: "Do not fear. You will give birth to a light which shall illumine the whole world." From her earliest childhood, prayer was Clare's only delight. She gave to the poor all the presents which she received from her parents. She despised all costly garments, all worldly pleasures. Beneath the fine clothes she was obliged to wear, she wore a rough hair-girdle. She partook of so little food that it seemed as if she wished to observe a continual fast. During this same period lived St. Francis, surnamed "the Seraphic," because of his great virtues. Clare frequently went to him and confided to him her desire to renounce the world and to consecrate her virginity to God, and to lead a perfect life in the most abject poverty. St. Francis who saw, that besides other gifts and graces, she was filled with the most ardent love of God, possessing great innocence of heart and despising the world, strengthened her in her holy desire, while at the same time he tested her constancy. Being sufficiently convinced that her desires were inspired by heaven, he advised Clare to leave her home, which she did on Palm Sunday, going to the church of the Portiuncula, where she had her hair cut off, as a sign that she would enter a religious life. She divested herself of all feminine ornaments, and attired in a penitential garb, tied around her with a cord, she was placed by St. Francis in a vacant Benedictine convent. She was at that time just eighteen years of age. When her parents heard of what she had done, they hastened to the convent, to take Clare home, declaring that this choice of a state of life was only a childish whim, or that she had been persuaded to it by others. Clare, however, after opposing their arguments, fled into the church, and clinging to the altar with one hand, with the other she bared her head shorn of its hair, exclaiming; "Know all, that I desire no other bridegroom than Jesus Christ. Understanding well what I was doing, I chose Him, and I will never leave Him." Astonished at this answer, all returned home, admiring her virtue and piety. Clare thanked God for this victory and was, because of it, more strengthened in her resolution. She had a sister younger than herself, named Agnes. A few days later she, too, fled from her parents' roof and going to Clare, wished to be invested in the same habit and to serve God in the same manner. St. Clare received her joyfully, but as all her relatives were provoked beyond measure that she, too, had entered a Convent, twelve of them went and forcibly tore her from her sister's arms. Clare took refuge in prayer, and as if inspired by the Almighty, ran after her sister, loudly calling her by name. God assisted her by a miracle. Agnes suddenly became immovable, as if rooted to the ground, and no one possessed strength enough to drag her from where she stood. Recognizing in this the powerful hand of God, they opposed her no longer, but allowed her to return to the convent. Meanwhile, St. Francis had rebuilt the old church of St. Damian and had bought the neighboring house. Into this house he placed his first two religious daughters, Clare and Agnes, who were speedily joined by others, desirous of conforming themselves to the rule of life which St. Francis had given to Clare. This was the beginning of the Order of Poor Clares, which has since given to the world so many shining examples of virtue and holiness, to the salvation of many thousands of souls. St. Clare was appointed abbess by St. Francis and filled the office for forty-two years with wonderful wisdom and holiness. Her mother also, together with her youngest daughter, took the habit and submitted to the government of St. Clare. The holy abbess enjoined on her order the most severe poverty, and when the pope himself offered her some property as an endowment, she humbly but earnestly refused to accept it. She was, to all in her charge, a bright example of poverty. In austerity towards herself she was more to be admired than imitated. The floor or a bundle of straw was her bed, a piece of wood, her pillow. Twice during the year, she kept a forty days' fast on bread and water. Besides this, three days of the week, she tasted no food, and so little on the others, that it is marvelous that she could sustain life with it. The greater part of the night she spent in prayer, and her desire for mortification was so great, that St. Francis compelled her to moderate her austerities. She nursed the sick with the greatest pleasure, as in this work of charity, she found almost constant opportunity to mortify and overcome herself. Besides all her other virtues, she was especially remarkable for her devotion to the Blessed Sacrament. She sometimes remained whole hours immovable before the tabernacle, and was often seen in ecstasy, so great was her love for the Savior it concealed. She sought her comfort in him alone in all her trials, amidst all her persecutions; and how great were the graces she thereby received, the following event will sufficiently illustrate.

The Saracens besieged Assisi and prepared to scale the walls of the Convent. St. Clare, who was sick at the time, had herself carried to the gates of the convent, where, with the ciborium, containing the Blessed Sacrament, in her hands, prostrating herself in company with all her religious, she cried aloud: " O Lord, do not give into the hands of the infidels the souls of those who acknowledge and praise Thee. Protect and preserve Thy handmaidens whom Thou hast redeemed with Thy precious blood." A voice was distinctly heard, saying:

"I will protect you always." The result proved that this was the voice of heaven. The Saracens, seized with a sudden fear, betook themselves to flight, those who had already scaled the walls, became blind, and flung themselves down. Thus were St. Clare and her religious protected and the whole city preserved from utter devastation by the piety and devotion of the saint to the Blessed Sacrament. We must omit many miracles which God wrought through his faithful servant, to relate her happy end. She had reached the age of sixty years, during twenty-eight of which she had suffered from various painful maladies, though she had not been confined to her bed, or rather, her bundle of straw. Her patience while suffering was remarkable, and she was never heard to complain of the severity or the duration of her sickness. The contemplation of the Passion of Christ made her own pains easy and even pleasing to her. "How short," said she one day, "seems the night to me, which I pass in the contemplation of the Lord's suffering!" At another time, she exclaimed: "How can man complain when he beholds Christ hanging upon the cross and covered with blood!" Having suffered so long and with such noble resignation, she saw at last, that her end was near. She received the Blessed Sacrament, and then exhorted all her daughters not to relax in their zeal to live in poverty and holiness. When her confessor conversed with her on the merits of patience, she said: "As long as I have had the grace to serve God in the religious state, no care, no penance, no sickness has seemed hard to me. Oh, how comforting it is to suffer for the love of Christ!" The hour of her death drew near, and she saw a great many white-robed virgins come to meet her, among whom was one who surpassed all the rest in beauty. She followed them, and they led her to see the Almighty face to face. Several who had read in the depths of her heart, said that she died more from the fervor of her love for God than from the effects of her sickness. Her holy death took place in 1253. The great number of miracles wrought after her death through her intercession, and the heroic virtues which made her so remarkable, induced Pope Alexander IV, only two years later, to place her in the number of saints.

Practical Considerations

"How can man complain when he beholds Christ hanging on the cross and covered with blood," asked St. Clare; and she also said that those nights in which she contemplated the passion of Our Lord, seemed short. During her long and painful maladies, she meditated on all the sufferings which Our Lord endured to save us, and by this means, learned such resignation that she not only had no thought of murmuring against Divine Providence but also bore her pains with great interior consolation. See your crucified Savior and think: "What is my suffering compared to that which my Redeemer endured for love of me? My Jesus has suffered with patience, with joy, and even with the desire to suffer still more. Why then should I be impatient and faint-hearted." With such thoughts you should animate yourself, especially during the night, as it is generally then that pains increase. Remember the night, the bitter night, which your Savior passed in the house of Caiaphas, maltreated in every possible manner, and pray for grace, to bear the cross laid upon you, with patience and fortitude. Only try it once and you will find great relief. St. Gregory said rightly: "Remembering the sufferings of Christ, we can bear everything patiently, how heavy it may be."

St. Clare, besides her love for her crucified Lord, had an especial devotion to the Blessed Sacrament. To it she went with all her cares and found strength and comfort. Why do you not do the same? If you had lived at the time when Christ was visible on earth and had known that he was truly the Savior, would you not have gone to him, full of faith and confidence, with all your troubles, and asked him for the graces you needed? Why are you not doing so now? Is he who is present in our churches under the form of bread, not the same who in times gone by, cured the sick and allowed no one to leave him without consolation? Your faith teaches you that he is the same. Why then do you not go to him with greater confidence? Why do you not look up to him for comfort and help? You so often speak of your needs to men, who either will not or cannot help you. What does it benefit you? Ah! go to the church; lay your heart bare before your Savior, represent to him all your perplexities, and he will comfort you. Especially when you are unhappy, in misfortune, in temptation, go to him. Pray to him in the words of St. Clare: "Lord, do not deliver to the demons the soul of one who believes in Thee. Protect and keep Thy servant whom Thou hast bought with Thy precious blood." Do not forget the instructions here given you. Follow the admonition of St. Paul, who says: "Let us therefore go with confidence to the throne of grace, that we may obtain mercy and find grace in seasonable aid" (Heb 5). This throne of grace you find in the Blessed Sacrament. Fly to it in all your sorrows, and you will find comfort and assistance.

Saint Teresa Benedicta of the Cross

The love of Christ was the fire that inflamed the life of St Teresa Benedicta of the Cross. Long before she realized it, she was caught by this fire. At the beginning she devoted herself to freedom. For a long time Edith Stein was a seeker. Her mind never tired of searching and her heart always yearned for hope. She traveled the arduous path of philosophy with passionate enthusiasm. Eventually she was rewarded: she seized the truth. Or better: she was seized by it. Then she discovered that truth had a name: Jesus Christ. From that moment on, the incarnate Word was her One and All. Looking back as a Carmelite on this period of her life, she wrote to a Benedictine nun: "Whoever seeks the truth is seeking God, whether consciously or unconsciously."[43]

Edith was born in 1891 to a Jewish family of Breslau, which was then in German territory. Her interest in philosophy, and her abandonment of the religious practice which she had been taught by her mother, might have presaged not a journey of holiness but a life lived by the principles of pure "rationalism." Yet it was precisely along the byways of philosophical investigation that grace awaited her: having chosen to undertake the study . . . she became sensitive to an objective reality. . . . This reality must be heeded and grasped above all in the human being, by virtue of that capacity for "empathy"—a word dear to her—which enables one in some way to appropriate the lived experience of the other. . . .

It was with this listening attitude that she came face to face, on the one hand, with the testimony of Christian spiritual experience given by Teresa of Avila and the other great mystics of whom she became a disciple and an imitator, and, on the

---

43 John Paul II, *Canonization of Edith Stein* (Holy See: Libreria Editrice Vaticana, 1998), http://w2.vatican.va/content/john-paul-ii/en/homilies/1998/documents/hf_jp-ii_hom_11101998_stein.html.

other hand, with the ancient tradition of Christian thought as consolidated in Thomistic philosophy. This path brought her first to Baptism and then to the choice of a contemplative life in the Carmelite Order. All this came about in the context of a rather turbulent personal journey, marked not only by inner searching but also by commitment to study and teaching, in which she engaged with admirable dedication. Particularly significant for her time was her struggle to promote the social status of women; and especially profound are the pages in which she explores the values of womanhood and woman's mission from the human and religious standpoint. . . .

Edith's encounter with Christianity did not lead her to reject her Jewish roots; rather it enabled her fully to rediscover them. But this did not mean that she was spared misunderstanding on the part of her family. It was especially her mother's disapproval which caused her profound pain. Her entire journey towards Christian perfection was marked not only by human solidarity with her native people but also by a true spiritual sharing in the vocation of the children of Abraham, marked by the mystery of God's call and his "irrevocable gifts" (cf. Rom 11:29).

In particular, Edith made her own the suffering of the Jewish people, even as this reached its apex in the barbarous Nazi persecution which remains, together with other terrible instances of totalitarianism, one of the darkest and most shameful stains on the Europe of our century. At the time, she felt that in the systematic extermination of the Jews the Cross of Christ was being laid on her people, and she herself took personal part in it by her deportation and execution in the infamous camp of Auschwitz-Birkenau. Her voice merged with the cry of all the victims of that appalling tragedy, but at the same time was joined to the cry of Christ on the Cross which gives to human suffering a mysterious and enduring fruitfulness. The image of her holiness remains forever linked to the tragedy of her violent death, alongside all those who with her suffered the same fate. And it remains as a proclamation of the Gospel of the Cross, with which she identified herself by the very choice of her name in religion.

Today we look upon Teresa Benedicta of the Cross and, in her witness as an innocent victim, we recognize an imitation of the Sacrificial Lamb and a protest against every violation of the fundamental rights of the person. We also recognize in it the pledge of a renewed encounter between Jews and Christians which, following the desire expressed by the Second Vatican Council, is now entering upon a time of promise marked by openness on both sides. Today's proclamation of Edith Stein as a Co-Patroness of Europe is intended to raise on this Continent a banner of respect, tolerance and acceptance which invites all men and women to understand and appreciate each other, transcending their ethnic, cultural and religious differences in order to form a truly fraternal society.[44]

Practical Considerations

A fearless search for truth led Edith Stein from unbelief to her impassioned love of Christ. The spiritual experience of Edith Stein is an eloquent example of this extraordinary interior renewal. A young woman in search of the truth has become a saint and martyr through the silent workings of divine grace: Teresa Benedicta of the Cross, who from heaven repeats to us today all the words that marked her life: "Far be it from me to glory except in the Cross of our Lord Jesus Christ."

St. Teresa of Avila

S aint Teresa, so greatly blessed by the Almighty, was born in 1515 at Avila, Spain, of pious and noble parents. Among other devotions, her parents frequently read pious books, and their daughter was taught to do the same as soon as she was able to read. Teresa soon became so much attached to this that she often retired with her brother to a solitary place to read more undisturbed.

---

44 John Paul II, *Spes Aedificandi, Proclamation of the Co-Patronesses of Europe* (Vatican: Libreria Editrice Vaticana, 1999), https://w2.vatican.va/content/john-paul-ii/en/motu_proprio/documents/hf_jp-ii_motu-proprio_01101999_co-patronesses-europe.html.

Though scarcely seven years of age she obtained so vivid a knowledge of worldly sufferings and spiritual peace that she sometimes would exclaim, as if in ecstasy: "O Eternity! To be tormented or rejoice for all eternity! Endless pain or endless joy! Oh, who can find words for it?" As she read the lives of the saints, her heart became so inflamed with the desire to honor Christ, that, in company with her brother, she secretly left home, intending to go to Africa to preach Christ among the Muslims. Although the two young adventurers were immediately pursued and brought back to their parents, the desire to die for Christ could not be torn from Teresa's heart.

At the age of twelve, Teresa lost her mother by an early death. She cast herself down before an image of the Blessed Virgin, and in a flood of tears, cried out: "Mother of Mercy! I choose thee for my Mother! Take me, a poor orphan, among the number of thy children!" The wonderful protection of the Queen of Heaven, which she enjoyed in the future, proved that her prayer was heard.

Without her mother's watchful eye, however, Teresa gradually abandoned her devout reading in favor of more worldly books. She grew cold in her devotion; she no longer found pleasure in prayer but became idle and vain. When her pious father noticed this change, he sent her into an Augustinian convent, where she soon came to see her fault and experienced bitter regret. She always thanked the special favor of Mary that she avoided great spiritual danger. Teresa began to read devout books again, which revived her pious zeal, which had almost entirely died out, in part because she had spent so much time in reading romances.

When she was twenty, she became dangerously sick, and her father took her home again. During her illness she recognized the vanity of the world and was filled with an intense desire to leave it entirely and to serve God in the religious state. Her father was greatly opposed to this, but she secretly fled to a convent of the Carmelite Nuns.

Teresa began her novitiate with great zeal, continued in it, and ended by taking upon herself the usual vows. Eventually, however, she once more lost her fervor in the service of God, because she conversed too long and too often with people of the world and thus neglected her prayers and lost her love for devout exercises. One day, going into church to pray, her eyes fell upon a picture of Our Savior representing him covered with wounds. At the same moment, her soul was deeply moved by the thought that Christ had suffered so much for her, and that she had been ungrateful and disobedient to him. Her heart became so filled with grief that it seemed to her as if it would break. Hence, sinking down before the image, she began to weep bitterly over her inconstancy, and said, with the most perfect trust: "Lord, I will not rise from the ground, until You have bestowed sufficient strength on me, not to sin in future, but to serve You faithfully and with my whole heart." This short but fervent prayer of Teresa was heard by the Almighty. Her heart was suddenly and forever changed; her love of God and her delight in prayer and other spiritual exercises were renewed. From that hour Teresa persevered, with increasing zeal, in the path of virtue and perfection.

God afterwards revealed to her that she owed her conversion to the intercession of St. Joseph and of the Blessed Virgin; hence she sought also to obtain the grace of perseverance by their aid. To this end, she represented frequently to herself the example of St. Magdalen and St. Augustine, and thus animated herself against a relapse. The faults of her past life filled her with sorrow, although according to the words of her confessors, she had not been guilty of great sin. In her eagerness to serve God most faithfully and to persuade others to do the same, Teresa determined to use all possible means, to institute once more the original austerity of the Carmelites, from which, by consent of the spiritual authorities, they had somewhat departed. God himself inspired her with these thoughts and promised her his aid in the execution of them. But as this was an undertaking which had never yet been attempted by a woman, it is easy to imagine the many and great obstacles she had to overcome.

Many of the Clergy and laity opposed her plans, and she was slandered and persecuted because of them. Nevertheless, heaven so visibly assisted her, that, before her death, she counted thirty-two new convents, either of men or of women, in which the religious of her order led a holy life in the observance of all the severity of the original rule. Whoever reflects on the trouble and labor it must have cost St. Teresa to carry out this great enterprise, will not hesitate to pronounce her success a great miracle. It is impossible to describe the great virtues of this holy foundress or the wonderful graces which God bestowed upon her. She possessed among others, the gifts of prophecy and of reading the secrets of the heart.

Perhaps because of her intimate experiences with death and illness, St. Teresa was always aware that this world is vain and fleeting. At the same time, the Lord constantly assured her of the permanence and beauty of heaven. During her prayer, she frequently fell into ecstasy, and was often seen surrounded by a divine light. Once she was heard to exclaim: "Ah! only one God! Only one death! Only one soul!" the explanation of which words she herself gave afterwards, as follows: "There is only one God; if we displease Him, there is no other from whom to seek help. Man dies only once; if therefore his death is unhappy, there is no chance left to remedy the mistake. One soul only do we possess; and if this is lost, there is no hope of salvation."

Teresa had many visions of our Lord, of the Blessed Virgin, St. Joseph, the holy Angels and other saints. In the last years of her life, seldom a day passed in which she was not favored with the sight of Christ in the holy Sacrament. The Divine Mother herself instructed, comforted, and strengthened her on all occasions. She said of St. Joseph, that she never asked anything of him which she did not obtain. But notwithstanding these and other great graces, her humility was so deep that she called herself the greatest of sinners, and desired to be considered as such. She often said that she owed it to the special grace of God that he treated her with mercy and not the just punishments she deserved. She was deeply humble, for she thanked God for every mercy he showed her.

St. Teresa was a serious thinker and writer. She holds a special place among mystical theologians, especially. Profound accounts of the spiritual life can be found in her autobiography, *Life of Teresa of Avila*, *The Way of Perfection*, and *The Interior Castle*.

Stories of other virtues, as her perfect obedience, her extreme poverty, her constant self-abnegation, her moderation in everything, and her great austerity, would fill volumes; but we must remember her love of God, as in this virtue she seems to have reached the highest point which a human being can attain. God was constantly in her thoughts even while she did other tasks. To him she constantly raised her heart by short interior prayers, which she sent to heaven with such fervency, that the flames of divine love which burned within her, were reflected on her countenance. The least fault she committed caused her many tears, and she made a vow, not only never to displease God by a voluntary venial sin, and to guard herself against every imperfection, but also constantly to endeavor to do what she knew was most agreeable to the Almighty.

It is most worthy of our admiration in the life of this saint, that she, though a weak person in many ways and almost always afflicted with sickness, could have written many books filled with more than human wisdom, worked so much for the honor of God and the salvation of souls, endured so many persecutions, wrongs, and slanders in her holy undertaking; and yet succeeded so well in what she had begun by divine inspiration. God manifested in her, what a feeble human being can do with his aid, and what great works he can perform through feeble hands. Because of her saintliness and learning, St. Teresa of Avila was named the first Doctor of the Church by Pope Paul VI.

Practical Considerations

The whole life of St. Teresa is filled with the most wholesome lessons. Let's notice some of them in a few words:

THE VALUE OF SPIRITUAL READING

Teresa began in early youth, following the teachings of her pious parents, to read devout books, and from this she first drew the spirit of piety. No sooner had she become interested in reading worldly books than she grew more indolent in the service of God. She did not return to her first fervor until she had resumed her pious reading.

As Christians we are called by God to a multitude of vocations. For those who are not living a religious vocation, it would be nearly impossible (and maybe even undesirable), to avoid all secular reading. Nevertheless, it is important for all of us to read spiritually nourishing books.

Foremost, of course, is the reading of Sacred Scripture. According to the *Catechism of the Catholic Church*, "The Church 'forcefully and specifically exhorts all the Christian faithful . . . to learn the surpassing knowledge of Jesus Christ, by frequent reading of the divine Scriptures. Ignorance of the Scriptures is ignorance of Christ.'"[45] Pope St. John Paul II reaffirms this when he writes that "an essential element of spiritual formation is the prayerful and meditated reading of the word of God (lectio divina), a humble and loving listening of him who speaks."[46]

Spiritual reading can be drawn from the writings of saints, and our faith can also be strengthened by reading doctors of the Church and other books which explain the teachings of the Church. Finally, surrounding yourself with literature with a Catholic

---

45 *Catechism of the Catholic Church*, no. 133.
46 Pope Saint John Paul II, Apostolic Exhortation *Pastores Dabo Vobis* (1992).

world view, such as Chesterton, Sigrid Undset, J. R. R. Tolkien wrote, can help us see the beauty of God's creation and his hand in everyday life.

PATRONAGE OF THE HOLY FAMILY

After the death of her mother, Teresa chose the Blessed Virgin to be another mother to her, and she sought and found in Mary comfort and help in all her needs. Through her intercession and that of St. Joseph, she received the grace of being constant in her efforts. Love Mary as your mother; seek consolation and help from her. St. Joseph should be one of your principal patrons, as his intercession is very powerful with the Almighty.

SINCERE LOVE AND SINCERE CONTRITION

St. Teresa dedicated her entire soul to prayer and would not have accomplished her great works without assistance. We should always pray when we undertake anything in our lives that it is in accord with the will of God. Teresa also had a very keen awareness of sinfulness. The sight of the wounded Jesus filled the heart of St. Teresa with great contrition for her former indifferent life; it inflamed her with true love of God and kept her until her end in these sentiments. When you consider how our Savior suffered for your sake, repent of your sins sincerely and take advantage of the gift of the sacrament of reconciliation.

WE ONLY HAVE ONE SOUL

There are many other lessons which the life of St. Teresa contains, and we can consider. Perhaps a place to begin is with the words she uttered in her ecstasy: "Only one God! Only one death! Only one soul!" Love this only God, and do not hurt him with your disobedience. Take earnest care of your only, your precious, your immortal soul.

WISDOM OF THE SAINTS

The Secret of Happiness According to a Holy Woman

If I were asked the secret of happiness, I should say self-forgetfulness and continual self-denial, which effectually destroy pride. The love of God should be strong enough to destroy all love for self.

BLESSED ELIZABETH OF THE TRINITY

He Wanted That We Love One Another

God loved the world so much that he gave his son and he gave him to a virgin, the blessed virgin Mary, and she, the moment he came in her life, went in haste to give him to others. And what did she do then? She did the work of the handmaid, just so. Just spread that joy of loving to service. And Jesus Christ loved you and loved me and he gave his life for us, and as if that was not enough for him, he kept on saying: Love as I have loved you, as I love you now, and how do we have to love, to love in the giving. For he gave his life for us. And he keeps on giving, and he keeps on giving right here everywhere in our own lives and in the lives of others.

It was not enough for him to die for us, he wanted that we loved one another, that we see him in each other, that's why he said: Blessed are the clean of heart, for they shall see God.

And to make sure that we understand what he means, he said that at the hour of death we are going to be judged on what we have been to the poor, to the hungry, naked, the homeless, and he makes himself that hungry one, that naked one, that homeless one, not only hungry for bread, but hungry for love, not only naked for a piece of cloth, but naked of that human dignity, not only homeless for a room to live, but homeless for that being forgotten, been unloved, uncared, being nobody to nobody, having forgotten what is human love, what is human touch, what is to be loved by somebody, and he says: Whatever you did to the least of these my brethren, you did it to me.[47]

ST. TERESA OF CALCUTTA

---

47 Mother Teresa, "Mother Teresa's Nobel Peace Prize Acceptance Speech," Transcript, Nobel Prize, December 10, 1979,

Confidence in God and His Grace

We know certainly that our God calls us to a holy life. We know that he gives us every grace, every abundant grace; and though we are so weak of ourselves, this grace is able to carry us through every obstacle and difficulty.

ST. ELIZABETH ANN SETON

Without the burden of afflictions, it is impossible to reach the height of grace. The gift of grace increases as the struggle increases.

ST. ROSE OF LIMA

You pay God a compliment by asking great things of him.

ST. TERESA OF AVILA

Humility Is Essential

Holiness does not consist in one exercise or another, but is a disposition of the heart, which renders us humble and little in the hands of

https://www.nobelprize.org/nobel_prizes/peace/laureates/1979/teresa-acceptance_en.html.

God, conscious of our weakness, and confident, even daringly confident, in His fatherly goodness.

ST. THERESE OF LISIEUX

Dear friend, show your gratitude to our Lord by becoming humble and obedient. Let us ask the Most Holy Virgin and the Holy Child Jesus for these two virtues for each other every day.

ST. BERNADETTE

Ah, how true it is that we love ourselves too much and proceed with too much human prudence, that we may not lose an atom of our consideration! Oh, what a great mistake that is! The saints did not act thus.

ST. TERESA OF AVILA

There is more value in a little study of humility and in a single act of it than in all the knowledge in the world.

ST. TERESA OF AVILA

In the Poorest We See Christ

One evening a gentleman came to our house and said, there is a Hindu family and the eight children have not eaten for a long time. Do something for them. And I took rice and I went immediately, and there was this mother, those little one's faces, shining eyes from sheer hunger. She took the rice from my hand, she divided into two and she went out. When she came back, I asked her, where did you go? What did you do? And one answer she gave me: They are hungry also. She knew that the next door neighbor, a Muslim family, was hungry.

What surprised me most, not that she gave the rice, but what surprised me most, that in her suffering, in her hunger, she knew that somebody else was hungry, and she had the courage to share, share the love. And this is what I mean, I want you to love the poor, and never turn your back to the poor, for in turning your back to the poor, you are turning it to Christ. For he had made himself the hungry one, the naked one, the homeless one, so that you and I have an opportunity to love him, because where is God? How can we love God? It is not enough to say to my God I love you, but my God, I love you here. I can enjoy this, but I give up. I could eat that sugar, but I give that sugar. If I stay here the whole day and the whole night, you would be surprised of the beautiful things that people do, to share the joy of giving. And so, my prayer for you is that truth will bring prayer in our homes, and from the foot of prayer will be that we believe that in the poor it is Christ. And we will really believe, we will begin to love. And we will love naturally, we will try to do something. First in our own home, next door neighbor in the country we live, in the whole world. And let us all join in that one prayer, God give us courage to protect the unborn child, for the child is the greatest gift of God to a family, to a nation and to the whole world. God bless you!

ST. TERESA OF CALCUTTA

Women in the Bible as Exemplars

People are scandalized that in these days the Lord deigns to magnify His great mercy in the frail sex. But why doesn't it cross their minds that a similar thing happened in the days of our fathers when, while men were given to indolence, holy women were filled with the Spirit of God so that they could prophesy, energetically govern the people of God, and even win glorious victories over Israel's enemies? I speak of women like Hilda, Deborah, Judith, Jael, and the like.[48]

ST. ELIZABETH OF SCHÖNAU

---

48 As quoted in Barbara Newman, *Sister of Wisdom: St. Hildegard's Theology of the Feminine* (Berkley: Univ. Of California Press, 1998), 39.

Do Not Put Off Striving for Holiness

Do not delay in serving your God. Walk in the way of His contemplation, like beloved daughters, with every humility and love and obedience, without murmuring, without detraction, without envy and similar things, but like young lambs pleasing to the living God.

ST. ELIZABETH OF SCHÖNAU

Our Lord Practiced All of the Most Excellent Kinds of Love

1. He loved us with a love of complacency, for His delights were to be with the children of men, and to draw man to Him, becoming man Himself.

2. He loved us with a love of benevolence, pouring His own divinity into man, in such a manner that man was made God.

3. He united Himself to us by a union so close and incomprehensible, that nothing was ever so closely united as the most holy divinity and humanity are now in the person of Our Lord.

4. He dissolved, as it were, His greatness, to reduce it to the form and figure of our littleness; whence He is called the fountain of living water, the rain and dew of heaven.

5. He fell into an ecstasy, not only, as St. Denis says, because, through the excess of His loving

goodness, He became in a manner out of Himself, extending His Providence to all things, and finding Himself in all; but also because, as St. Paul says, He quitted Himself, emptied Himself, laid aside His glory and grandeur, descended from the throne of His incomprehensible majesty, and, so to speak, annihilated Himself, in order to arrive at our humanity, to replenish us with His divinity, to overwhelm us with His goodness, to elevate us to His dignity, and to bestow on us the divine existence of children of God; and that expression which has been so often used : I live, saith the Lord, He has been able to repeat in the language of His Apostle: I live, now not I, but man liveth in me; my life is man, and to die for man is my gain; my life is hidden with man in God. He who dwelt in Himself wishes henceforward to dwell in us; He who had lived from unbeginning ages in the bosom of His Eternal Father becomes mortal in the womb of His temporal Mother; He who had eternally been God becomes Man for eternity; to such a degree has God been ravished and drawn into an ecstasy, through love for man.

6. He loved us to admiration, as shown in the cases of the Centurion and the Cananaean woman.[49]

7. He lovingly contemplated the young man who had observed the commandments from his youth, and desired to know the way to perfection.

---

49 Mt 8:5–13; 15:21–28.

8. He took a loving rest among us, and sometimes with suspension of the senses, as in the womb of His Mother, and during His infancy.

9. He had tenderness towards little children, whom He took in His arms and lovingly caressed, towards Martha and Magdalen, towards Lazarus over whom He wept, as also over the city of Jerusalem.

10. He was animated with an extraordinary zeal, which, as St. Denis says, made Him jealous: turning away, as far as lay in Him, all evil from His loved human nature, even at the risk and peril of His own life; banishing the devil, the prince of this world, who appeared as His rival and competitor.

11. He had a thousand thousand loving sufferings; from which proceeded those divine words: I have a baptism wherewith I am to be baptized, and how I am straitened until it be accomplished! He foresaw the hour of being baptized in His own blood, and languished for its arrival, the love He bore us pressing Him to see us delivered by His death from eternal death. Thus He was sorrowful even to a bloody sweat in the Garden of Olives, not only through the bitter grief He felt in the inferior part of His soul, but also through the immense love He bore us in the rational part: the one giving Him a horror of death, the other an extreme desire of it: so that between this horror and this desire He suffered a most cruel agony, even to a great effusion

of blood, which flowed as from a fountain, trickling down upon the ground.

12. Finally, this divine lover died in the midst of the flames of holy love, because of the infinite charity He bore towards us, and by the force and efficacy of love, that is to say, He died in love, by love, for love, and of love. For, though the cruel torments were more than sufficient to cause the death of any one, yet death could not enter into the life of Him who held the keys of life and death, unless divine love had first opened the gates to death, allowing it to enter and to plunder His divine body of life: love not being content with having made Him mortal for us, if it did not also see Him die. It was by election, and not by compulsion, that He died. No one taketh away my life, He says, but I lay it down of myself; I have power to lay it down, and to take it up again. He was offered, says Isaias, because he willed it; and therefore it is not said that His spirit departed, or separated itself from Him, but on the contrary that He gave up His spirit, breathed it out, and placed it in the hands of His Eternal Father. Accordingly, St. Athanasius remarks that He bowed down his head to die, thereby to consent to the approach of death, which otherwise could not dare touch Him; and, crying out with a loud voice, He surrendered His spirit to His Father, to show that as He had sufficient strength and breath not to die, yet He had so much love that He could no longer live without vivifying by His death those who otherwise could never

avoid death, or attain to true life. On this account, the death of the Savior was a true sacrifice, and a holocaustic sacrifice, which He Himself offered to His Father, for our redemption. "While the pains and sufferings of His Passion were so great and excessive that any other person would have died of them, yet, as far as regarded Him, He never would have died of them if He had not willed it, or if the fire of His infinite charity had not consumed His life. He was then the high-priest who offered Himself to His Father, and He immolated Himself in love, to love, by love, for love, and of love.

Beware, however, of thinking that this loving death of the Savior happened after the manner of a rapture. The object for which His charity led Him to death was not so amiable as to ravish His divine soul to it. No, His soul quitted His body after the manner of an ecstasy, pushed and impelled by love, as we see myrrh pouring out its first liquor from abundance alone, without being pressed or drawn in any way. This accords with what He Himself has said, as already remarked: No one takes away or ravishes my life from me, but I lay it down voluntarily. O God! what a furnace to inflame us to the performance of the exercises of holy love for a Savior so good, seeing that He so lovingly performed them for us who are so bad! The sweet charity of Jesus Christ presses us![50]

---

50 Francis de Sales, *The Consoling Thoughts of St. Francis de Sales* (Dublin: M.H. Gill and Son, 1892), 56.

Imitate Him

We become what we love and what we love shapes what we become. If we love things, we become a thing. If we love nothing, we become nothing. Imitation is not a literal mimicking of Christ, rather it means becoming the image of the beloved. . . . This means we are to become vessels of God's compassionate love for others.

ST. CLARE OF ASSISI

How to Preserve Peace of Soul in Time of Trial

Nothing disturbs us so much as self-love and self-esteem. If our heart does not overflow with tender emotions, if our mind does not teem with sublime sentiments, if our soul is not flooded with exquisite sweetness, we are sad; if anything difficult is to be done, if any obstacle opposes our just plans, behold us in a state of haste to have it overcome, and we are overcome ourselves by the haste. Why is this so? Undoubtedly, because we are too much attached to our comfort, our ease, our convenience. We would wish to say our prayers in perfume, and practice heroic virtue eating sugar-cake; but we do not consider the meek Jesus, prostrate on the earth, sweating blood, through the dreadful combat that rages in His interior, between the feelings of the inferior part of His soul and the resolutions of the superior part.

Hence it happens that when we fall into any fault or sin, we are astonished, troubled, and impatient. We only desire consolations and are unwilling to blame our misery, our weakness, or our nothingness. Were we to do a few things, we would find peace: let us have a pure intention to seek the honor and glory of God on all occasions; let us perform the little we can for this object, according to the advice of our spiritual director, and leave the rest to God. Why should a person who has God for the object of his intentions, and who does what he can, torment himself? Why should he trouble himself? What has he to fear? No, no—God is not so terrible to those who love Him! He is content with a little, for He knows that we have not much.

And know that Our Lord is called in Scripture the Prince of Peace, and hence, wherever He is absolute Master, He preserves peace. It is nevertheless true, that, before establishing peace in any place, He first makes war there, separating the heart and soul from their dearest and most intimate affections, such as immoderate love of one's self, confidence and complacency in one's self, and other like evils. When Our Lord separates us from these cherished and favorite passions, it seems as if He ripped our living heart, and we are filled with the most bitter sentiments; we can hardly prevent our whole soul from discussing its misfortune, so sensible is this separation.

But all this agitation is not inconsistent with peace, when, though almost submerged by desolation, we still keep our will resigned to that of Our Lord, nailed to His divine good-pleasure, and not quitting our duties, but fulfilling them courageously. Our Lord gives us an example in the Garden of Gethsemane; for, overwhelmed inside and out, He resigned His heart to His Father's will, saying: not my will, but thine be done, and ceased not, great as was His anguish, to visit and admonish His disciples. To preserve peace in the midst of war, and sweetness in the midst of bitterness, is indeed worthy of the Prince of Peace.

From what I have just said, I desire you to draw three conclusions:

- first, that we often imagine peace to be lost, because we are in pain, while it is not lost, as may easily be known by the fact that we still wish to renounce ourselves, to depend on the good-pleasure of God, and to fulfil the duties of our state;
- second, that we must of necessity endure interior pain, while God tears away the last remnant of the old man, to renovate us in the new man who is created according to God, and therefore we should not be troubled, or suppose that we have fallen into disgrace with Our Lord;

- third, that all those thoughts which cause vexation and agitation of mind do not come from God, who is the Prince of Peace, but are temptations of the enemy, and therefore to be rejected and disregarded.

How to Preserve Peace of Soul Continued

Humility enables us to view our imperfections undisturbed, remembering those of others. For why should we be more perfect than others? In like manner, it enables us to view the imperfections of others without trouble, remembering our own. For why should we think it strange that others have imperfections, when we have them ourselves? Humility makes our heart meek towards the perfect and the imperfect, towards the former through reverence, towards the latter through compassion. Humility helps us to receive sufferings meekly, knowing that we deserve them, and favors reverently, knowing that we do not deserve them. As to the exterior, I suggest that you make some act of humility every day, either in word or deed: I mean by words coming from the heart, such as words humbling you to an inferior; indeed, as by performing some little office or service for the house or for individuals.

I dread the unreasonably screwed-up spirit of restraint and melancholy. No, I desire you to have a great and generous heart in the service of Our

Lord, yet to be humble, meek, and sincere. Lacking this, our imperfections, which we view so narrowly, trouble us much, and are thus retained; for nothing preserves them better than anxiety and uneasiness to remove them.[51]

ST. FRANCIS DE SALES

Patience in Suffering

If there be a true way that leads to the Everlasting Kingdom, it is most certainly that of suffering, patiently endured.

ST. COLETTE

I realized that if all went well, I would not have had the opportunity to love Jesus. And I am so happy.

BLESSED CHIARA BADANO

If you suffer with him, with him you will reign, grieve with him, with him you will rejoice, die with him on the cross of tribulation, with him you will possess mansions in Heaven among the splendors of the saints.

ST. CLARE OF ASSISI

---

51   Francis de Sales, 122–25.

Always keep your faith in the love of God. If you have to suffer, it will be because you are deeply loved. So whatever happens, love and chant your thanksgiving.

BLESSED ELIZABETH OF THE TRINITY

Sin is the cause of all this pain; but all shall be well, and all shall be well, and all manner of things shall be well.

ST. JULIAN OF NORWICH

Edith Stein on the Education of the Souls of Women

The emotions have been seen as the center of woman's soul. For that reason, emotional formation will have to be centrally placed in woman's formation. Emotion exists in sentiments such as joy and sorrow, moods such as cheerfulness and gloom, attitudes such as enthusiasm and indignation, and dispositions such as love and hate. Such emotional responses demonstrate the conflict of the individual with the world and also with himself. It is only the person who is deeply involved with life whose emotions are stirred. Whoever is aiming to arouse emotion must bring it into contact with something which will hasten this involvement. Above all, these are human destinies and human actions as history and literature present them to the young—naturally, this will be contemporary events as well. It is beauty in all its ramifications and the rest of the aesthetic categories. It is truth which prompts the searching human spirit into endless pursuit. It is everything which works in this world with the mysterious force and pull of another world. The subjects which are especially affective in emotional training are religion, history, German, and possibly other languages if the student succeeds in overcoming the external linguistic difficulties and is able to penetrate to the spiritual content.

But, generally speaking, it is not enough only to stir the emotions. An evaluating factor exists in all emotional response. What the emotions have grasped are viewed as being either positively or negatively significant, either for the concerned individual himself or, independent of him, viewed in the significance of the object in itself. It is thereby possible for the emotional responses themselves to be judged as being "right" or "wrong," "appropriate" or "inappropriate." It is a matter of awakening joyful emotion for authentic beauty and goodness and disgust for that which is base and vulgar. It is important to guide the young person to perceive beauty and goodness, but this is not sufficient. Often the child is first awakened to the value of things by his awareness of the adult's responses—above all, that of the teacher—enthusiasm inspires enthusiasm. The guidance of attitudes is simultaneously a method of training the ability to discriminate. One cannot introduce him only to the good and the beautiful: life will also bring him into contact with ugliness, and by then the child should have already learned to differentiate between the positive and the negative, the noble and the base, and to learn to adapt himself in suitable ways. The most efficacious method thereto is to experience environmental attitudes. The attitude of the developing individual towards the world depends greatly on environmental influences which are both arbitrary and instinctive. And thus it is of extraordinary significance that the child's education be placed in the hands of people who themselves have received proper emotional formation.

However, this most essential, even indispensable, method of emotional formation through value judgments is accompanied by a certain danger as well: feelings and emotional attitudes are "contagious"; they are easily picked up by one person from another. These attitudes are, indeed, but pure predispositions in the affected soul. In the first place, the mind is not open to the values presented; and these sentiments, moreover, are neither momentarily or generally vital. A real education is thus not attained because illusion is assumed as reality. Hence there is need for education relevant to the authenticity of sentiments, the differentiation of appearance from reality both in the environment and in one's own soul. This is not possible without sufficient intellectual training. Intellect and emotion must cooperate in a particular way in order to transmute the purely emotional attitudes into one cognizant of values. (It is not our concern here to demonstrate this method of cooperation.) Whoever knows exactly why something is good or beautiful will not simply assume the attitudes of another. And then the exercise of this intellectual critique develops the ability to distinguish between spiritual truth and falsehood. Emotional reactions invoke action. The authentic art lover will gladly sacrifice comfort for the sake of artistic enjoyment. Those who truly love their neighbor will not be unsympathetic and apathetic to their neighbor's need. Words should inspire action; otherwise, words are mere rhetoric camouflaging nothingness, concealing merely empty or illusory feelings and opinions.[52]

EDITH STEIN (ST. TERESA
BENEDICTA OF THE CROSS)

Work and Holiness

The first end I propose in our daily work is to do the will of God; secondly to do it in the manner he wills it; and thirdly to do it because it is his will.

ST. ELIZABETH ANN SETON

---

52 Edith Stein, *Essays on Woman*, ed. Lucy Gelber and Romaeus Leuven, trans. Freda Mary Oben (ICS Publications, 2017).

Jacob did not cease to be a saint because he had to attend to his flocks.

ST. TERESA OF AVILA

A Clear Conscience

When God will be your judge, He will require no better witness, than your own conscience.

ST. AUGUSTINE

Keep Watch

St. Bonaventura tells us, that there is no greater loss, than the loss of time.

ST. PHILIP NERI

On Loving Our Enemies

Notice the Gospel. Is this not the commandment? A new commandment, says the Lord, give I unto you, that you love one another.[53] — In this we know that we are in Him, if in Him we be perfected. Perfected in love, he calls them: what is perfection of love? To love even enemies, and love them for this purpose, that they may be

---

53 "I give you a new commandment, that you love one another. Just as I have loved you, you also should love one another" (Jn 13:34).

brothers and sisters. This is not a carnal love. To wish a man worldly good, is good; but if that fails, let the soul be safe. Do you wish life to any that is your friend? You do well. Do you rejoice at the death of your enemy? You do badly. But you do not know if the life you wish your friend is good for him, or if the death you rejoice at for your enemy harms him. It is uncertain whether this present life be profitable to any person or unprofitable: but the life which is with God without doubt is profitable.

So, love your enemies as to wish them to become your brothers and sisters; so, love your enemies as that they may be called into your fellowship. For He who, hanging on the cross, said, Father, forgive them, for they know not what they do, loved in this way.[54] For He did not say, Father let them live long; indeed, they kill me, but let them live. No, He was casting out eternal death from them, by His most merciful prayer, and by His most surpassing might.[55]

St. Augustine

---

54 Luke 23:34.
55 Philip Schaff, ed., "Homily 1 on the First Epistle of John," in *Augustine: Homilies on the Gospel of John; Homilies on the First Epistle of John; Soliloquies,* trans. H. Browne, vol. 7, *A Select Library of the Nicene and Post-Nicene Fathers of the Christian Church,* First Series (Buffalo: Christian Literature Co., 1886), http://www.newadvent.org/fathers/170201.htm.

Avoid Anger and Impatience

There is no sin nor wrong that gives a man such a foretaste of hell in this life as anger and impatience.

ST. CATHERINE OF SIENA

Love Makes Us Beautiful

Let us love, because He first loved us.[56] For how should we love, except He had first loved us? By loving we became friends: but He loved us as enemies, that we might be made friends. He first loved us and gave us the gift of loving Him. We did not yet love Him: by loving we are made beautiful.

As the love increases in you, so the loveliness increases: for love is itself the beauty of the soul.[57]

ST. AUGUSTINE

---

56 "We love because he first loved us" (1 Jn 4:19).

57 Philip Schaff, ed., "Homily 9 on the First Epistle of John," in *Augustine: Homilies on the Gospel of John; Homilies on the First Epistle of John; Soliloquies*, trans. H. Browne, vol. 7, A Select Library of the Nicene and Post-Nicene Fathers of the Christian Church, First Series (Buffalo: Christian Literature Co., 1886), http://www.newadvent.org/fathers/170201.htm.

Too Late Did I Love You, O Beauty!

Too late did I love You, O Beauty, so ancient, and yet so new! Too late did I love You! For look, You were within me, and I was searching for you outside of myself. I rushed heedlessly among the things of beauty You made. You were with me, but I was not with You. Those outside things kept me far from You, which, unless they were in You, were not. You called, and cried aloud, and forced open my deafness. You gleamed and shine and chase away my blindness. You exhaled odors, and I drew in my breath from You. I tasted and indeed hunger and thirst. You touched me, and I burned for Your peace.[58]

ST. AUGUSTINE

Right Here, Right Now

As to the past, let us entrust it to God's mercy, the future to divine providence. Our task is to live holy the present moment.

ST. GIANNA BERETTA MOLLA

---

58 Philip Schaff, ed., "Confessions," in *The Confessions and Letters of St. Augustine*, trans. J. G. Pilkington, vol. 1, A Select Library of the Nicene and Post-Nicene Fathers of the Christian Church, First Series (Buffalo: Christian Literature Co., 1886), chap. 10, http://www.newadvent.org/fathers/170201.htm.

To the Servant of God . . . every place is the right place, every time the right time.

ST. CATHERINE OF SIENA

Maintain an Eternal Perspective Amid the Here and Now

We must often draw the comparison between time and eternity. This is the remedy of all our troubles. How small will the present moment appear when we enter that great ocean.

ST. ELIZABETH ANN SETON

Concerning Gossip

Gossip is a disease that infects and poisons the apostolate. It goes against charity, means a waste of energy, takes away peace and destroys one's union with God.[59]

ST. JOSEMARIA ESCRIVA

Call it by its name: grumbling, gossiping, back-biting, mischief making, tale-bearing, scandal-mongering, intrigue . . . , slander . . . , treachery?

---

59 Josemaria Escriva, "Opus Dei - Writings of the Founder," accessed July 31, 2018, http://www.escrivaworks.org/book/furrow.

Self-appointed critics sitting in judgment easily end up as "gossiping old maids"!

ST. JOSEMARIA ESCRIVA

Gossip is a very human thing, they say. And I reply: we have to live in a divine manner.

ST. JOSEMARIA ESCRIVA

The evil or flippant word of only one man can create a climate of opinion, and even make it fashionable to speak badly about somebody. . . . Then that thin mist of slander rises from below, reaches a high level and perhaps condenses into black clouds.

—But when the man persecuted in this way is a soul of God, the clouds shower down a beneficial rain, come what may; and the Lord ensures that he is exalted by the very means with which they tried to humiliate or defame him.

ST. JOSEMARIA ESCRIVA

Envy

Envy is a gnawing pain which springs from the success and prosperity of another; and this is the reason why the envious are never free of trouble and vexation. If an abundant harvest fills the granaries of a neighbor, if success crowns his efforts, the envious man is chagrined and sad. If one man can boast of prudence, talent, and eloquence; if another is rich, and is very generous to the poor; if good works are praised by all around, the envious man is shocked and grieved.

The envious, however, dare not speak; although envy makes them pretend to be glad, their hearts are sore within. If you ask him what vexes him, he dare not say the reason. It is not really the happiness of his friend that annoys him, neither is it his gaiety that makes him sad, nor is he sorry to see his friend prosper. But he is convinced that the prosperity of others is the cause of his misery.

This is what the envious would be forced to acknowledge, if they spoke the truth sincerely; but because they dare not confess so shameful a sin, they, in secret, torture themselves and let it ruin their peace.

As the shadow ever accompanies the pedestrian when walking in the sun, so envy throws its shadow on those who are successful in the world.[60]

ST. BASIL

---

60 Charles Kenny and W. T. Gordon, *Half-Hours with the Saints and Servants of God: Including Biographical Notes and Many Translations* (London: Burns and Oates, 1882), 265–66.

On Flattery

Nothing so corrupts the heart and mind as flattery, for the flatterer's tongue does more harm than the persecutors sword. We are dragged downwards by an evil which is inherent within us, we feel favorably towards those who flatter us, and although in our reply we show, or pretend to show, that we are unworthy of their praise, we nevertheless receive the flattering praise with a secret joy and pleasure.[61]

ST. JEROME

On Vanity

I ask vain women, do you not tremble at the thought that, when our Lord and Savior shall come to judge the living and the dead, He will bid you leave His presence for evermore, and that He will reproach you like this? "Depart from Me, you are not My work, and I cannot see the least resemblance to your former self. The paint, powder, false curls, and other vain applications have so altered and disguised you, that I cannot recognize that you once belonged to Me!"[62]

ST. CYPRIAN

---

61 Kenny and Gordon, 270.
62 Modified from Kenny and Gordon, 288.

Moderation

Excessive eating and drinking have killed many a person, moderation has killed no one; too much wine has injured many a healthy person, temperance has never done any harm. Many have died right at the banquet, falling over from their heated blood.[63]

ST. AMBROSE

Lies

When the tongue says one thing, and the heart means another; this is deceit, and a lie. If through humility you circulate a lie, even if you had not committed a sin of lying before, you become, by lying, what you were not before, a sinner. The sin of lying is not only committed by word of mouth, but by deeds designedly carried out for the purpose of deceiving.

It is a lie to call yourself a Christian, when you do not practice the works of Jesus Christ.

ST. AUGUSTINE

---

63 Modified from Kenny and Gordon, 298.

Love Your Neighbor as Yourself

About the commandment to love our neighbor as ourselves, St. Bernardine of Sienna, remarks, that we should love our neighbor with a genuine affection, and not in the same way as we love things necessary or useful, such as bread, a house, and other things which are for our use or for our amusement; these we do not love as ourselves, but for ourselves.

St. Chrysostom says that when the Son of God gave us the best of prayers, He did not intend that we should say "My Father" but, Our Father; inasmuch, as we have a common Father in heaven we should consider all men as our brethren, and that in this way we should love each other with a mutual love, with a love stronger in grace than in nature, as the same hope of a heavenly reward.

St. Bernard says, that he who does not love God, cannot love his neighbor with a sincere affection; God therefore must be our first love, in order that we may be able to love our neighbor, in God and for God.

St. Philip Neri tells us, that in dealing with our neighbor, we must assume as much pleasantness of manner as we can, and by this friendliness, win him to the way of virtue.

Loving Your Enemies

It is more glorious to bear silently an insult in imitation of Christ than to come back with a sharp and sarcastic reply.

If it should happen that the memory of an injury stirs up your soul to anger, call to mind what the Son of God has suffered for us and how comparatively few have been your sufferings. By this means, you will throw water on the smoldering flames and you will be better enabled to smother your resentment.

ST. GREGORY OF NAZIANZEN

Poverty in itself is not a virtue; but the love of poverty is so. Jesus Christ has said, "Blessed are the poor in spirit," not those who possess nothing.

ST. BERNARD

To Married Persons

It is honorable to all persons, in all persons, and in all things, that is, in all its parts. To all persons, because even virgins ought to honor it with humility; in all persons, because it is equally holy in the rich and poor; in all things, because its origin, its end, its advantages, its form, and its matter are all holy. It is the nursery of Christianity, which supplies the earth with faithful souls, to complete the

number of the elect in heaven; in a word, the pres-
ervation of marriage is of the highest importance to
the commonwealth, for it is the origin and source of
all its streams.

Would to God that his most beloved Son were
invited to all marriages, as he was to that of Cana.
. . . Above all things, I exhort married people to that
mutual love which the Holy Spirit so much recom-
mends in the Scripture. You that are married! I tell
you not to love each other with a natural love, for it
is thus that the turtles love; nor do I say, love one
another with a human love, for the heathens do this;
but I say to you, after the great Apostle, "Husbands,
love your wives, as Christ also loved the Church."
And you, wives, love your husbands, as the Church
loves her Savior. It was God that brought Eve to our
first father, Adam, and gave her him in marriage;
it is also God, O my friends! who, with his invisible hand, has tied the knot of the holy bond of your
marriage, and given you to one another; why do you
not, then, cherish each other with a holy, sacred,
and divine love?

St. Francis De Sales

Passing the Faith to Children

St. Monica, being pregnant of the great St.
Augustine, dedicated him by frequent obla-
tions to the Christian religion, and to the service

and glory of God, as he himself testifies, saying, that "he had already tasted the salt of God in his mother's womb." This is a great lesson for Christian women, to offer up to his divine Majesty the fruit of their wombs, even before they come into the world; for God, who accepts the offerings of a humble and willing heart, commonly at that time seconds the affections of mothers; witness Samuel, St. Thomas of Aquin, St. Andrew of Fiesola, and many others. The mother of St. Bernard, a mother worthy of such a son, as soon as her children were born, took them in her arms, and offered them up to Jesus Christ; and, from that moment, she loved them with respect as things consecrated to God and entrusted by him to her care. This pious custom was so pleasing to God that her seven children became afterwards eminent for sanctity. But when children begin to have the use of reason, both fathers and mothers ought to take great care to imprint the fear of God in their hearts.

ST. FRANCIS DE SALES

Good Works, However Small

When we neglect nothing and are careful to store up the little gains we can make, we shall insensibly increase our riches; it is nearly the same with spiritual riches.

Since our Divine Lord and Judge will keep an account of a glass of water, there is no good action we ought to despise, however small it may appear, and we must not be grieved if we cannot do great things; little things naturally are the forerunners of great actions. Neglect the former, and you will not be capable to do the latter.

It was to prevent this misfortune that Jesus Christ has promised to reward us for little things.

There is nothing easier than visiting a sick person, nevertheless, God has fixed a great reward for this good work, however easy it may appear.

ST. JOHN CHRYSOSTOM

Holiness does not demand anything great, beyond the ability of the person. It depends on God's Love; every daily act can be transformed into an act of love.

ST. URSULA JULIA LEDOCHOWSKA

On Loving Our Neighbors as Ourselves

About this commandment, St. Bernardine of Sienna remarks that we should love our neighbor with a genuine affection, and not in the same way as we love things necessary or useful, such as bread, a house, and other things which are for our use or for our amusement; these we do not love as ourselves, but for ourselves.

The More Love You Give, the More You Owe

The love of our neighbor, says St. Paul, is a debt which is not discharged in the ordinary way; that is to say, a debt once paid, is paid once for all. This is what St. Paul means, we are always beholden in the love we are obliged to have for one another.

The more you pay in love and charity, the more you will owe, says St. Augustine.

St. Philip Neri tells us that in dealing with our neighbor, we must assume as much pleasantness of manner as we can, and by this affability, win him to the way of virtue.

Accepting an Insult

It is more glorious to bear silently an affront, in imitation of Christ, than to retort with a sharp and sarcastic reply. If the remembrance of an injury stirs up your soul to anger, call to mind what the Son of God has suffered for us, and how comparatively few have been your sufferings. By this means, you will throw water on the smoldering flames, and you will be the better enabled to smother your resentment.

St. Gregory of Nazianzen

Prayer Is Essential

Prayer places our understanding in the brightness and light of God. Prayer exposes our wills to the heat of heavenly love. There is nothing that so frees our understanding from ignorance or our will from its bad inclinations, as prayer. Prayer is the water of benediction, which makes the plants of our good desires grow green and flourish. It washes our souls from their imperfections and quenches the thirst of passion in our hearts. But, above all, I recommend mental and familiar prayer, and particularly that which has the life and passion of our Lord for its object. By making Him the frequent subject of your meditation, your whole soul will be replenished with Him; you shall learn His form better and shape all your actions according to His model. As He is the light of the world, it is then by Him, in Him, and for Him that we ought to acquire shine and be enlightened. He is the tree of desire, under whose shadow we ought to refresh ourselves. He is the living fountain of Jacob, in which we may wash away all our stains.

In short, as little children, by hearing their mother talk, lisp at first but eventually learn to speak her language; so we, by keeping close to our Savior by meditation, and observing His words, actions, and affections, shall, by the help of His grace, learn to speak, to act, and to will, like Him.

ST. FRANCIS DE SALES

The great method of prayer is to have none. If in going to prayer, one can form in oneself a pure capacity for receiving the spirit of God, that will suffice for all methods.

ST. JANE FRANCES DE CHANTAL

The stillness of prayer is the most essential condition for fruitful action. Before all else, the disciple kneels down.

ST. GIANNA BERETTA MOLLA

We must pray without ceasing, in every occurrence and employment of our lives, that prayer which is rather a habit of lifting up the heart to God in a constant communication with Him.

ST. ELIZABETH ANN SETON

How often I failed in my duty to God, because I was not leaning on the strong pillar of prayer.

ST. TERESA OF AVILA

I would never want any prayer that would not make the virtues grow within me.

ST. TERESA OF AVILA

On Reacting to Anger

Meekness preserves within us the image of God, but anger blots it out. If any hard or cutting words should inadvertently escape from your lips, apply the remedy and cure, from the same mouth that caused so sensitive a wound.

ST. AUGUSTINE

We must accustom ourselves to perform all our actions with quiet serenity; force of habit can correct or tame the most stubborn bad temper. But because sometimes we are naturally so quick to anger, it is difficult to offer an immediate cure. Perhaps we should reflect on the motives for our impatience, in order to lead us gradually to a cure.

When strong passions come upon us so suddenly that there is no time for reflection, we must at least try to soothe them if we cannot immediately master them. It is sometimes proper to make a desperate effort; but is more sensible to try to conquer by degrees, more especially when the first bursts of impatience or anger assail us. It is recommended in scripture; give time for anger to evaporate, and then extinguish it entirely. We must not only do what we can to prevent our getting angry, but we must use greater efforts to subdue it when it does come on. Never answer an angry person with arrogant haste; if he or she be bad-tempered, why fall into the same fault? When two flinty stones are quickly rubbed together, sparks will fly out.

If you cannot cure anger by those means which a calmer judgment would suggest, you must have recourse to clever schemes. Patience is a great assistant, for time softens the most violent passion. If we are continually provoked by a person who is always having recourse to sharp, impertinent answers, and we feel that we have not enough command over our own temper, we can, at least, moderate our tongue by keeping silent. Holy Scripture gives us this advice: "Suffer in silence, and do not have recourse to sharp retorts." You can later seek reconciliation and do your best to make it lasting.

If you have not the strength of mind to not take offence, you can bridle your tongue and allow no bitter reply to escape your lips. When you have taken all such precautions, you will find that more is to be done to secure a mild and even temper.

ST. AMBROSE

A Few Maxims From St. Teresa of Avila

- Man's mind is like good ground which, left untilled, grows thorns and thistles.
- Talk little when with many people.
- Be modest in all your words and actions.
- Never contend much, especially about trifles.
- Speak with quiet cheerfulness to everyone and never ridicule.
- Correct others prudently, humbly and with self-abasement.
- Think before you speak, recommending your words earnestly to our Lord that you may say nothing displeasing to Him.
- Never affirm anything of the truth of which you are uncertain.
- Unless charity requires, do not obtrude your opinion unasked.
- It is a great help to the soul to perform all your actions as if you saw God present.
- Look upon yourself as the servant of all: see Christ in others and you will show them respect and reverence.
- Accustom yourself to make frequent acts of love, which inflame and melt the soul.
- Be indulgent to others, but rigorous to yourself.
- Examine your conscience in all your actions and at all times, endeavoring by the grace of

God to amend the failings you discover: in that way you will attain perfection.

- Do not reflect on other people's faults, but on their virtues and your own defects.
- Be mindful of the sentiments with which our Lord inspires you during prayer, and act upon the desires He then gives you.
- Recognize the providence and wisdom of God in all created things and praise Him for them.
- To the soul that can endure, any life will easy seem; any life a living death the impatient soul will deem.
- He who seeks no private gain always finds things to his mind: He who would his comfort find ever sees reason to complain.
- When for earthly things I sigh, then, although I live, I die!

Written on St. Teresa's Bookmark

Nada te turbe.
Let nothing disturb you;
Nor frighten you ever;
All things are passing;
But God changes never.
Patience attains.
With God as your own
Nothing is lacking.

On Faith

Faith is a lamp which gives us spiritual light and warmth.[64]

ST. THOMAS AQUINAS

Hold in your hand the lantern of Faith; and let the flame of Charity shine from it, to show you what you must do, and what you must avoid.

ST. AUGUSTINE

A tree cannot grow without roots; a building cannot be raised without a foundation; every river must flow from a source. So the Christian life and virtues can neither exist nor flourish, nor become a source of life, unless they proceed from faith.

ST. AUGUSTINE

As a vessel that has no anchor is tossed about by the wind, so our mind, when not anchored to Faith, is continually agitated by the wind of human opinions and doctrines.

ST. GREGORY THE GREAT

---

64 *The Catholic Church, the Teacher of Mankind* (New York: Office of Catholic Publications, 1905).

A virtuous life is to the soul what food is to the body. For as our body cannot live without food, so Faith cannot subsist without good works.

ST. JOHN CHRYSOSTOM

On Hope

Wait upon the Lord, be faithful to His commandments, and He will elevate your hope and put you in possession of His Kingdom. Wait upon Him patiently, wait upon Him by avoiding all sin. He will come, do not doubt it; and in the approaching day of His visitation, which will be that of your death and His judgment, He will Himself crown your holy hope. Place all your hope in the Heart of Jesus. It is a safe asylum, for he who trusts in God is sheltered and protected by His mercy. To this firm hope, join the practice of virtue, and even in this life you will begin to taste the unspeakable joys of Paradise.

ST. BERNARD

We must have confidence in God, who is what He always has been. We must not be disheartened because things turn out contrary to our wishes.

ST. PHILIP

A servant of God should fear nothing, not even Satan, who is soon thwarted when made little account of. If the Lord is mighty, the demons are but his bond-slaves; what evil therefore can they do to the servants of so great a King?

ST. TERESA OF AVILA

God is so good and so merciful, that to obtain Heaven it is sufficient to ask it of Him from our hearts.

ST. BENEDICT JOSEPH LABRE

As a mother delights in taking her child on her knees, in caressing and feeding him, so does our God delight in treating with love and tenderness those souls who give themselves entirely to Him, and place all their hopes in His goodness and bounty.

ST. ALPHONSUS LIGUORI

On Charity

In the royal galley of Divine Love, there is no galley slave; all the rowers are volunteers.

ST. FRANCIS DE SALES

Since our Lord dwells in our soul, his prayer is ours, and I desire to partake of it unceasingly, keeping like a little pitcher beside the fountain, so that I may be able to give life to others by letting his inexhaustible streams of charity overflow on them.

BLESSED ELIZABETH OF THE TRINITY

He who does not acquire the love of God will scarcely persevere in the grace of God, for it is very difficult to renounce sin, merely through fear of scolding and punishment.

ST. ALPHONSUS LIGUORI

Charity is the sweet and holy bond which links the soul with its Creator; it binds God with man and man with God.

Everything comes from love. All is ordained for the salvation of man. God does nothing without this goal in mind.

ST. CATHERINE OF SIENA

Under the influence of fear, we bear the Cross of Christ with patience; under the more inspiring influence of hope, we carry the Cross with a firm

and valiant heart; but under the consuming power
of love, we embrace the Cross with passion.

ST. BERNARD

God has loved us from all eternity. Children of
men, says the Lord, remember that I first loved you.
You had not yet been born, the world itself did not
exist, and even then I loved you. As long as I am
God, I have loved you; I have loved you as long as I
have loved Myself.

ST. ALPHONSUS LIGUORI

What a weakness it is to love Jesus Christ only
when He caresses us, and to turn cold immediately
He afflicts us. This is not true love. Those who love
in this way, love themselves too much to love God
with all their heart.

ST. MARGARET MARY ALACOQUE

Be Merry

Be merry, really merry. The life of a true
Christian should be perpetual jubilee, a pre-
lude to the festivals of eternity.

ST. THEOPHANE VENARD

WISDOM FROM TODAY'S CATHOLIC WOMEN

The Feminine Genius

But this woman, (with the alabaster jar who anoints Jesus: see Mk 14:3–9, ed.) with her feminine genius, recognized the absolute priority of love for the person of Jesus himself. Her gesture is a prophetic word for the church: before all else that we do, we minister to him first. All social action, all that we do for the poor, is secondary—in fact, our service to others is fruitful only to the degree that we first and foremost serve him. . . .

In this case he says, "And truly, I say to you, wherever the gospel is preached in the whole world, what she has done will be told in memory of her" (Mark 14:9). It is a solemn pledge: her gesture will always be remembered as an essential part of the good news, exemplifying the perfect response to Jesus' laying down of his life on the cross. Her act of love is a proclamation of the gospel! It will lead many others to do what she did—to "waste themselves" on Jesus, without counting the cost. This woman illustrates the natural gift that women have of seeing others with the heart, of empathy with them, of affirming what is truly valuable. Women have a deep awareness of the logic of the gospel, so different from human calculations. This is the great gift that women are called to bring to the new evangelization today.

Here there is a deep irony: by Jewish law, women were disqualified from being witnesses because they were considered unreliable. But at the empty tomb, only the women are present. They are the first witnesses to Christ's resurrection, the crowning moment of his victory over sin and death.

Jesus overturns that law! In fact, he puts women at the forefront of the church's mission; he makes a woman an "apostle to the apostles." He says to Mary Magdalene, "Go to my brethren and say to them, I am ascending to my Father and your Father, to my God and your God" (John 20:17). Today more than ever, the world urgently needs women to fulfill their unique mission—to be at forefront of the new evangelization, pouring themselves out without counting the cost, affirming the value of others, and calling all human beings to their own deepest vocation to love.[65]

DR. MARY HEALY

---

65 Mary Healy, *The Marian Style: The Feminine Genius in Evangelization*. Delivered at the Congress of Ecclesial Movements and New Communities Rome, Nov. 20–22, 2014. http://www.laici.va/content/dam/laici/documenti/donna/bibbia/english/Marian%20Style%20-%20Feminine%20Genius%20in%20Evangelization.pdf .

Mulieris Dignitatem boldly asserts that love is the meaning of life and that women are first or "prior" in the "order of love," the first to be "entrusted" with new life (29–30), to acknowledge the presence of, to nourish, and to nurture, life. It bases its conclusions not only upon the fact of women's fertility, but also upon women's demonstrated gifts for acknowledging persons. This last is a source of real knowledge, alongside Revelation and the structures of our created bodies.

. . . This feature of Mulieris Dignitatem—its claim that women are gifted with a capacity for the person, and its simultaneous insistence that loving service is the meaning of life, "upends" the entire historical inclination to account feminine traits as lesser, both because they are feminine, and because the ranking assumes that worldly goods and power are the measure of success, rather than the capacity to love well. . . .

. . . Still, for the most part, governments have asked women and children and families to make the greater sacrifices if they wish to have children, rather than enabling women and men to put their families first if they are also working outside the home. Governments have rather emphasized women's freedom not to have children or to have fewer children via contraception and abortion. Leading feminist groups have adopted the same priorities. Both governments and self-described women's groups need to be called to account for this. The opportunity costs of these priorities are the dearth of policies in most—though not all—countries which value the caretaking work of full-time at-home mothers, or the caretaking work of mothers and fathers working also outside the home.[66]

HELEN ALVARE

Let us be honest with ourselves, however. We are not talking about some obscure principle of astrophysics. The so-called unintelligible principle of Humanae Vitae might be summed up quite simply as this: sex = strengthened conjugal unity + babies.

From this perspective, the struggle between man and woman resulting from original sin (cf. Genesis 3:16) points to a battle within each human heart: a struggle between—as George Weigel puts it—"love and lust, between self-mastery and self-assertion, between freedom as giving and freedom as taking, which is often at the expense of the woman."

As for us Christians in the married state, we are called to live the radical demands of Christian love.[67]

MICHELE M. SCHUMACHER

---

66 Helen Alvare, Excerpts from presentation entitled *Changes in the Image of Women in History* given at the seminar "God entrusts the human being to woman" in Rome, October 2013.

67 Michele M. Schumacher, *A Plea for Human Ecology: on the Prophetic Value of Humanae Vitae for today.* http://www.laici. va/content/dam/laici/documenti/donna/teologia/english/ humanae-vitae2%20-%20M%20Schumacher.pdf .

Motherhood is so important that the Church can never see it as just an optional extra, a biological experience, a burden or a hobby. A mother has a particular dignity of her own, a particular status, extraordinary responsibilities, the greatest of joys. To be a mother is one of the most basic and natural of longings, and it is a terrible distortion of reality to see it as merely a lifestyle choice.

In the recent past we have perhaps too often simply taken for granted the women saints, but it's time to take a good look at the great range of them. There they are, from the very earliest days—greeting the risen Lord in the Garden, suffering death in Rome's Colosseum rather than deny their faith in him, giving themselves in service to the Church and to the poor and sick and lonely and imprisoned. As mystics and missionaries, heroic martyrs and courageous founders of religious orders, in public life as sovereigns or in quiet service in convent or school, the Church's women saints are testimony to the fact that Mother Church takes legitimate pride in her daughters. And, no, she doesn't think that they are of less worth than her sons. She sees and rejoices in the complementarity of the two sexes, knowing—and teaching—that this is part of God's plan, not to be downplayed or ignored, much less regarded as a nuisance.[68]

JOANNA BOGLE

---

68 Joanna Bogle, FAITH Magazine, May – June 2011), http://

A woman's vocation to motherhood emanates in all her relationships whether she is a mother physically, spiritually, or both. The mystery and beauty of a woman is unequivocally tied to the fact that she bears life.

Woman has a special mission that is unique only to her. She is at the center of a great battle: a battle for man's heart and the true meaning of our bodies and authentic beauty.

This war that has been waged on the woman's body, her beauty and life itself should be of no surprise to us as Christians. The ProtoEvangelium, Genesis 3:15, warned us of this: "I will put enmity between you and the woman, and between your offspring and hers; they will strike at your head, while you strike at their heel." Mary is the woman, but in her femininity all women are encompassed. God restored our fallen nature and Mary became the new Eve. We are to emulate Mary as women. It is through this imitation of Mary that we also, together with her, receive the mission to "strike at evil's head." Simply by living out authentic femininity with joy, we unquestionably begin to extinguish the effects of counterfeit beauty. Furthermore, in living out genuine motherhood in all its aspects, whether biological or spiritual, we also help to begin snuffing out the culture of death that at times

www.laici.va/content/dam/laici/documenti/donna/teologia/
english/contemporary-catholicism-on-femininity.pdf.

seems to be taking over our world. Beauty is powerful and a woman's beauty is even more powerful because she has been given the unique gift and extraordinary beauty of bringing about life.[69]

ALEJANDRA M. CORREA

69 Alejandra M. Correa, "The Beauty of Woman," http://www. laici.va/content/dam/laici/documenti/donna/culturasocieta/ english/Beauty%20of%20Woman%2006-15-2014%20PCL.pdf.

10

PRAYERS

PRAYERS FOR FAMILIES

Prayer for the Family

ord God, from You every family in heaven and on earth takes its name. Father, You are Love and Life. Through Your Son, Jesus Christ, born of woman, and through the Holy Spirit, fountain of divine charity, grant that every family on earth may become for each successive generation a true shrine of life and love.

Grant that Your grace may guide the thoughts and actions of husbands and wives for the good of their families and of all the families in the world.

Grant that the young may find in the family solid support for their human dignity and for their growth in truth and love.

Grant that love, strengthened by the grace of the sacrament of marriage, may prove mightier than all the weakness and trials through which our families sometimes pass.

Through the intercession of the Holy Family of Nazareth, grant that the Church may fruitfully carry out her worldwide mission in the family and through the family. Through Christ our Lord, who is the Way, the Truth and the Life. Amen.

POPE ST. JOHN PAUL II

Prayer of Parents for Their Children

O heavenly Father, I entrust my children to You. Be their God and Father. Mercifully supply whatever I lack through weakness or neglect. Strengthen them to overcome the corruptions of the world, to resist the temptations of evil, whether from within or without; and deliver them from the secret snares of the enemy. Pour Your grace into their hearts, and confirm and multiply in them the gifts of thy Holy Spirit, that they may daily grow in grace and in the knowledge of our Lord Jesus Christ; and so, faithfully serving You here, may come to rejoice hereafter; through the merits of the same Jesus Christ, who with thee and the Holy Spirit lives and reigns forever. Amen.

Morning Prayer for Mothers

M ost merciful God, You have given me this day so that I may serve You and work out my salvation by being faithful to my duties in life.

Assist me, then, with Your grace. Above all, help me to perform with care and fidelity the most important and sacred duties which I owe to my children. Allow me to go before them with the light of good example. Bless whatever I may do or say on this day for their education.

Take my children under the protection of Your love and grace. Shield them from danger and keep them far from all evil. Preserve them from sin. Fill their tender hearts with Your holy love. Awaken them, that they may serve You faithfully, growing in grace and virtue as they grow in age.

Holy guardian angels, and patron saints of my children, take care of them and pray for them. Amen.[70]

Evening Prayer for Mothers

Thanks be to You, O my God and my Father, for all the graces and favors which You have bestowed on me and on my children today. All good gifts proceed from You and You rule over us with mercy. I am saddened, O Lord, by my ingratitude to

70 Modified from W. Cramer and J. P. M. Schleuter, *The Christian Mother; The Education of Her Children and Her Prayer. With an Account of the Archconfraternity of Christian Mothers* (New York; Cincinnati; Chicago: Benziger Brothers, 1880), 162, http://libraryaccess.bac.edu:2198/title/christian-mother-the-education-of-her-children-and-her-prayer-with-an-account-of-the-archconfraternity-of-christian-mothers/oclc/17311162&referer=brief_results.

You, the best of Fathers! In Your mercy pardon me, especially for any sins I have committed as a mother. I renew my promises to You; hasten to help me with the riches of Your grace. Expand my heart with true charity for my children. May I always be filled with holy earnestness in the education of my children, and in whatever concerns their true welfare.

Father, I commend to You my children during this night. May Your hand defend them during their night's rest. Drive far away from their place of rest any evil. Let their holy angels be near to them. Preserve them in innocence. Holy Virgin, St. Joseph, holy angels, and all you Saints in heaven, please pray for my children. Amen.[71]

A Prayer of a Mother for Her Children

Assist me O heavenly Father, with the many challenges presented by duty to my children. Give me true Christian discretion, so that I may see what to grant, what to deny, and let neither passion, nor bad mood, nor over-fondness make me yield to them in anything that will harm them in either soul or body. Enable me always to give them good examples, to protect them from ill company and from hearing or seeing what may tempt them to evil. When they do stray, may I correct them in a timely manner out of love and never in passion.

---

71 Modified from Cramer and Schleuter, 163–64.

Deliver me from all manner of wasteful spending, from all intemperance, idleness, vanity, or any neglect or poor management that may hinder me from providing for their comfortable subsistence in this life. At the same time, deliver me from preparing them for unhappiness, by being too solicitous to make them too worldly.

Direct me, O God, in all that can contribute to their Christian education; help me to remove from them all that may do them harm. Deliver me from any unjust favoritism, from discouraging them, or showing any unreasonable anxiety, lest they seek unwholesome remedies for the troubles they find at home. Be a Father to them, and supply, by Your goodness, whatever is wanting in me. Preserve them against the corruption of the world, of sin, and all evil, and move them to all good. Deliver them from the effects of a vain and fickle mind, and make them always Your faithful children here, that they may come at length to that happiness which Christ has purchased for them. Amen.

Prayer for the Grace to Be a Good Example

O God, what powerful encouragement Your divine Son gives to me when He says, "Let your light shine." It is Your holy will that I should be for my children the example of a life pleasing to You. How else can they become virtuous themselves? I ask, therefore, for Your assistance, through the merits gained for us by Your son, to lead a truly Christian life. Enrich me with Your grace, that I may be able to avoid in all my words, actions, and omissions what is unworthy of a Christian. Help me to exercise all the virtues of a Christian life, and to grow in perfection, so that my life may be an example for my children.

What wonders You have worked in Your Saints! Watch over me too and graciously protect me. I am indeed not worthy of such great graces, but You are a merciful God. You love my children since they are also Your children. For their sake and that of Jesus, Your Son, grant my petitions. Amen. [72]

For a Wife

O God who has ordained for me the vocation of marriage, give me grace to perform its obligations as a Christian should. Preserve my love unblemished according to Your command. Give me the grace to work for the good of my marriage, for without Your grace I cannot succeed.

Allow me the judgment to manage all circumstances for the best of our family. Grant a true love between my husband and myself to foster peace in our home. Give me the moderation to yield in my own inclinations and ways when I should and the courage to stand firm when I must, and the wisdom

---

72 Modified from Cramer and Schleuter, 175–76.

to know what is best. Whatever the challenges, may I be of good cheer, never yielding to weakness, impatience, or ill humor, or anything that would weaken our holy bond, for I know that we are to part only in death.

May I always be faithful and persevere under the difficulties and responsibilities of my vocation, doing and suffering whatever comes to me with true submission to Your will. Strengthen me so that, in times of calm or trouble, through ways which are easy or hard, I may remember to make the best use of my abilities, remembering always Your desire that I to work out my salvation with diligence.

PRAYERS OF GRATITUDE

S aying a blessing before a meal is a small thing, and something we may do without thinking. Yet when we are aware of what we are doing, the smallest of things can be occasions to bring a family closer to God and one another. It is fitting, of course, to give thanks for the blessings of God after a meal as well.

Grace Before Meals

B less us, O Lord, and these gifts, which we are about to receive from thy bounty, through Christ our Lord. Amen.

Grace After Meals

We give thee thanks, O Almighty God, for these and all thy blessings, through Christ our Lord. Amen.

HOW TO MAKE A NOVENA

One of the essential qualities of prayer is perseverance, as is evident from the words of St. James, who says that "the prayer of the righteous is powerful and effective" (Jas 5:16). On the eve of his Passion, our divine Lord gave us in his own example of being steadfast; as Saint Matthew tells us: "So leaving them again, He went away and prayed for the third time, saying the same words" (Mt 26:44). For these reasons the Church has long approved the practice of praying for certain periods to ask some favor or blessing which we desire of our Father in heaven.

The Church has many special times for prayer, such as the holy seasons of Lent and Advent. Also, there are special kinds of devotions. One such devotion, commonly called a novena, is said regularly for nine days. Sometimes, novenas are prayed to honor one of the three Divine Persons, such as the novena of the Seven Gifts of the Holy Spirit. Other novenas are prayed to saints by whose favor with

God we hope with confidence to obtain our cherished request.

A novena consists of certain prayers or devotions continuing for nine days. The days may be in succession or they may be for one special day of the week for nine successive weeks. No set forms of prayers are required.

Since a state of grace is one of the surest means of partaking of God's blessings, anyone making a novena should try to receive the sacraments of Penance and Holy Eucharist as often as possible during the nine weeks; or, if the novena is made for nine consecutive days, the sacraments should be received worthily sometime before the last day of the devotions.

Fruitful prayer requires faith in God's promises, hope in his goodness, steadfastness, and resignation to his Divine Will. This is the prayer of which Christ spoke when he said: "Very truly, I tell you, if you ask anything of the Father in my name, he will give it to you" (Jn 16:23). A novena offers us a wonderful way to spend seek the blessings of the lord.

Novena to Saint Ann

Prayer to Saint Ann

O glorious Saint Ann, you are filled with compassion for those who invoke you, and with love for those who suffer. Heavily burdened with the weight of my troubles, I cast myself at your feet and humbly beg of you to take the present intention, which I recommend to you in your special care.

Please recommend it to your daughter, the Blessed Virgin Mary, and place it before the throne of Jesus, so that he may bring it to a happy issue.

Continue to intercede for me until my request is granted. But above all obtain for me the grace one day to see my God face to face, and with you and Mary and all the saints to praise and bless him for all eternity. Amen.

Our Father . . .

Hail Mary . . .

Glory be . . .

Invocation

Saint Ann, help me now and at the hour of my death!

Good Saint Ann, intercede for me!

First Day

Dear Saint Ann, I appeal to you and place myself under your great motherly care as I begin this novena in your honor. Please listen to my prayers and requests.

Help me, also, to begin this time of prayer with a heart open to the loving grace of God. Give me the strength to begin a new life that will last forever.

Finally, blessed Saint Ann, I ask you to recommend me to your daughter, the most holy virgin Mary. Through her, may I receive the spirit of prayer, humility, and the love of God.

> Take time to reflect on this. Now say the prayer to Saint Ann, followed by the Our Father, Hail Mary, and Glory Be. Finish with the invocation: Saint Ann, help me now and at the hour of my death! Good Saint Ann, intercede for me!

Second Day

From the depths of my heart, good Saint Ann, I offer you my homage and I ask you to shelter me under the mantle of your motherly care. Help me to purify my thoughts and desires.

Aid my decisions that all that I do may be done in love.

Reflection, Prayer to Saint Ann, etc.

Third Day

Good Saint Ann, you were the first to respond to the needs of Mary, the mother of our Savior. You watched over her in her infancy, presented her at the temple, and consecrated her to the service of God.

By the great power God has given you, show yourself to be my mother and consoler. Help me dedicate myself to God and to my neighbors.

Console me in my trials and strengthen me in my struggles.

Reflection, Prayer to Saint Ann, etc.

Fourth Day

Good Saint Ann, you offered your daughter in the temple with faith, piety, and love. With the happiness which then filled your heart, help me to present myself to God and to the world as a committed disciple of Jesus. Take me under your protection. Strengthen me in my temptations. Show yourself to be a mother and help me to live a life of holiness and love.

Reflection, Prayer to Saint Ann, etc.

Fifth Day

Good Saint Ann, by God's special favor, grant consolation to us who invoke you. Help us to grow in spiritual wealth for the life to come and guide us in our temporal affairs as well. Grant us the gift of continuous conversion and renewal of heart. Help us to accept the Gospel of Jesus over and over again so that we may be ready to be true disciples in whatever situations we may experience during our lives.

Reflection, Prayer to Saint Ann, etc.

Sixth Day

Good Saint Ann, free my heart of pride, vanity, and self-love. Help me to know myself as I really am, and to learn meekness and simplicity of heart. I realize God's great love for me. Help me to reflect this love through works of mercy and charity toward my neighbor.

Reflection, Prayer to Saint Ann, etc.

Seventh Day

Good Saint Ann, by the power and grace God has placed in you, extend to me your helping hand. Renew my mind and heart. I have unbounded confidence in your prayers. Direct my actions according to your goodness and wisdom. I place myself under your motherly care. Pray that I may receive the grace to lead a devout life on earth, and that I may obtain the everlasting reward of heaven.

Reflection, Prayer to Saint Ann, etc.

Eighth Day

Saint Ann, you gave birth to Mary, whose divine Son brought forth salvation to our world by conquering death and restoring hope to all people. Help me to pray to him who, for love of us, clothed himself with human flesh. May I be guided from anything that is displeasing in the sight of God. Pray that the Spirit of Jesus may enlighten and direct me in all I do. Good Saint Ann, keep a watchful eye on me. Help me bear all my crosses and sustain me with courage.

Reflection, Prayer to Saint Ann, etc.

Ninth Day

Good Saint Ann, I have come to the end of this novena in your honor.

Do not let your kind ear grow weary of my prayers, though I repeat them so often. Implore for me from God's providence all the help I need to get through life. May your generous hand bestow on me the material means to satisfy my needs, and to alleviate the plight of the poor. Good Saint Ann, pray that I may praise and thank the Holy Trinity for all eternity.

Reflection, Prayer to Saint Ann, etc.

MARIAN PRAYERS

Hail, Holy Queen! (Salve, Regina)

Hail, holy Queen, Mother of mercy, our life, our sweetness and our hope. To thee do we cry, poor banished children of Eve. To thee to we send up our sighs, mourning and weeping in this valley of tears. Turn, then, most gracious advocate, thine eyes of mercy toward us, and after this, our

exile, show unto us the blessed fruit of thy womb,
Jesus. O clement, O loving, O sweet Virgin Mary.

V. Pray for us, O holy Mother of God.
R. That we may be made worthy of the promises
of Christ.

Let us pray:
Almighty and everlasting God, Who by the
working of the Holy Spirit didst prepare both body
and soul of the glorious Virgin Mother, Mary, that
she might deserve to be made a worthy dwelling for
Thy Son, grant that we who rejoice in her memory,
may, by her loving intercession, be delivered from
present evils and from lasting death, through the
same Christ our Lord. Amen.

Queen of Heaven (Regina Caeli)

V. Queen of Heaven, rejoice, alleluia.
R. For He whom you did merit to bear, alleluia.
V. Has risen, as he said, alleluia.
R. Pray for us to God, alleluia.
V. Rejoice and be glad, O Virgin Mary, alleluia.
R. For the Lord has truly risen, alleluia.

Let us pray:
O God, who gave joy to the world through the
resurrection of Thy Son, our Lord Jesus Christ, grant
we beseech Thee, that through the intercession of

the Virgin Mary, His Mother, we may obtain the joys of everlasting life. Through the same Christ our Lord. Amen.

Hail, O Queen of Heaven (Ave, Regina Caelorum)

Welcome, O Queen of Heaven.
   Welcome, O Lady of Angels
Hail! thou root, hail! thou gate
From whom unto the world, a light has arisen:
Rejoice, O glorious Virgin,
Lovely beyond all others,
Farewell, most beautiful maiden,
And pray for us to Christ.

V. Allow me to praise thee, O sacred Virgin.
R. Against thy enemies give me strength.

Grant unto us, O merciful God, a defense against our weakness, that we who remember the holy Mother of God, by the help of her intercession, may rise from our iniquities, through the same Christ our Lord. Amen.

Litany of Our Lady of Sorrows

Lord, have mercy on us.
Christ, have mercy on us.
Lord, have mercy on us.

Christ, hear us.
Christ, graciously hear us.

God, the Father of heaven, have mercy on us.
God the Son, Redeemer of the world, have
      mercy on us.
God the Holy Spirit, have mercy on us.
Holy Trinity, One God, have mercy on us.

Holy Mary, Mother of God, pray for us.
Holy Virgin of virgins, pray for us.
Mother of the Crucified, pray for us.
Mother most sorrowful, pray for us.
Mother most tearful, pray for us.
Mother afflicted, pray for us.
Mother forsaken, pray for us.
Mother bereft of thy Son, pray for us.
Mother pierced with the sword, pray for us.
Mother consumed with grief, pray for us.
Mother filled with anguish, pray for us.
Mirror of patience, pray for us.
Rock of constancy, pray for us.
Joy of the afflicted, pray for us.
Ark of the desolate, pray for us.
Refuge of the abandoned, pray for us.
Shield of the oppressed, pray for us.
Conqueror of the incredulous, pray for us.
Solace of the wretched, pray for us.
Medicine of the sick, pray for us.
Help of the faint, pray for us.

Strength of the weak, pray for us.

Haven of the shipwrecked, pray for us.

Calmer of tempests, pray for us.

Companion of the sorrowful, pray for us.

Treasure of the Faithful, pray for us.

Theme of Prophets, pray for us.

Staff of the Apostles, pray for us.

Queen of Martyrs, pray for us.

Light of Confessors, pray for us.

Pearl of Virgins, pray for us.

Comfort of Widows, pray for us.

Joy of all Saints, pray for us.

Pray for us, most Sorrowful Virgin,
That we may be made worthy of the promises of Christ.

Lamb of God, that takest away the sins of the
world, Spare us, O Lord.

Lamb of God, that takest away the sins of the
world, Hear us, O Lord.

Lamb of God, that takest away the sins of the
world, Have mercy upon us.

Let us pray:

Imprint, O Lord, thy wounds upon our hearts,
that we may read therein sorrow and love; sorrow
to endure all suffering for thee; love to despise all
love but thine; who lives and reigns, world without
end. Amen.

O God, in whose Passion, according to the prophecy of Simeon, a sword of grief pierced through the most sweet soul of Thy glorious Blessed Virgin Mother Mary: grant that we, who celebrate the memory of her Sorrows, may obtain the happy effect of Thy Passion, Who lives and reigns world without end. Amen.

Angelus

V. The Angel of the Lord brought tidings to Mary.
R. And she conceived by the Holy Spirit.
Hail Mary, etc.

V. Behold the handmaid of the Lord.
R. Let it be to me according to your word.
Hail Mary, etc.

V. And the Word was made Flesh.
R. And dwelt among us.
Hail Mary, etc.

V. Pray for us, O holy Mother of God.
R. That we may be made worthy of the promises of Christ.

Let us pray:
Lord, Pour Your grace into our hearts, that as we have whom Incarnation of you Son Jesus Christ by the message of an angel, so by His cross and

passions may we be brought to the glory of His Resurrection. Through Christ Our Lord. Amen.

Memorare

Remember, O most gracious Virgin Mary, that never was it known that anyone who fled to your protection, implored your help or sought your intercession was left unaided. Inspired with confidence, I fly to you, O virgin of virgins, my Mother. To you I come, before you I stand, sinful and sorrowful. O Mother of the Word Incarnate, despise not my petitions, but in your mercy, hear and answer me. Amen.

To Our Lady of Guadalupe

O Immaculate Virgin, Mother of the true God and Mother of the Church!, who from this place reveal your clemency and your pity to all those who ask for your protection, hear the prayer that we address to you with filial trust, and present it to your Son Jesus, our sole Redeemer.

Mother of Mercy, Teacher of hidden and silent sacrifice, to you, who come to meet us sinners, we dedicate on this day all our being and all our love. We also dedicate to you our life, our work, our joys, our infirmities and our sorrows. Grant peace, justice and prosperity to our peoples; for we entrust to your care all that we have and all that we are, our

Lady and Mother. We wish to be entirely yours and to walk with you along the way of complete faithfulness to Jesus Christ in His Church; hold us always with your loving hand.

Virgin of Guadalupe, Mother of the Americas, we pray to you for all the Bishops, that they may lead the faithful along paths of intense Christian life, of love and humble service of God and souls. Contemplate this immense harvest, and intercede with the Lord that He may instill a hunger for holiness in the whole people of God, and grant abundant vocations of priests and religious, strong in the faith and zealous dispensers of God's mysteries.

Grant to our homes the grace of loving and respecting life in its beginnings, with the same love with which you conceived in your womb the life of the Son of God. Blessed Virgin Mary, protect our families, so that they may always be united, and bless the upbringing of our children.

Our hope, look upon us with compassion, teach us to go continually to Jesus and, if we fall, help us to rise again, to return to Him, by means of the confession of our faults and sins in the Sacrament of Penance, which gives peace to the soul.

We beg you to grant us a great love for all the holy Sacraments, which are, as it were, the signs that your Son left us on earth.

Thus, Most Holy Mother, with the peace of God in our conscience, with our hearts free from evil and hatred, we will be able to bring to all true joy and true peace, which come to us from your son, our Lord Jesus Christ, who with God the Father and the Holy Spirit, lives and reigns for ever and ever. Amen.

POPE ST. JOHN PAUL II

Our Lady of Guadalupe, Mystical Rose

Our Lady of Guadalupe, Mystical Rose,
make intercession for holy Church,
protect the sovereign Pontiff,
help all those who invoke you in their
    necessities,
and since you are the ever Virgin Mary
and Mother of the true God,
obtain for us from your most holy Son
the grace of keeping our faith,
of sweet hope in the midst of the bitterness of
    life
of burning charity, and the precious gift
of final perseverance.

POPE ST. PIUS X

To Our Blessed Lady, for the Salvation of My Soul

Hail, O most holy and blessed Virgin, full of grace!

Mirror of beauty and loveliness, of whom and by whom it pleased our Savior Jesus Christ, the Son of God, the King of heaven, the brightness of his Father's glory, to be born and nourished—Obtain for me, O blessed Lady, from your only begotten Son, whatever you know to be necessary for the salvation of my soul. Holy Mother of God, assist me this day, and the remainder of my life, in all my difficulties, temptations, and dangers, but especially at the hour of my death, graciously say you will be near me, that, by you prayers and protection, I may be safe in that last and dangerous battle. Amen.

Commemoration of the Seven Joys of Our Blessed Lady in Heaven

1. Rejoice, O Spouse of the Holy Ghost, for the bliss which you possess in paradise, where you are exalted above the angelic choirs. Hail Mary . . .

2. Rejoice, O true Mother of God, for the happiness which you feel in paradise; for as the sun illuminates the earth, so do you, with your divine Son, adorn and illuminate heaven by your brightness. Hail Mary . . .

3. Rejoice, O Daughter of God, for the joy to which you have attained in paradise, where the whole hierarchy of angels and archangels, thrones and dominations, and all the blessed, pay you honor, acknowledging you as the Mother of their Creator. Hail Mary . . .

4. Rejoice, O Handmaid of the blessed Trinity, for the gladness which you feel and enjoy in paradise; for all the graces which you ask from your divine Son are instantly granted, and because, as St. Bernard says, "no grace is granted to us on earth which has not first passed through your holy hands." Hail Mary . . .

5. Rejoice, O Queen of heaven, for you alone deserve to sit at the right hand of your divine Son, who is seated at the right hand of the eternal Father. Hail Mary . . .

6. Rejoice, O hope of sinners, refuge of the unhappy, for the bliss which you enjoy in paradise; for the eternal Father rewards with his most precious graces all those who love and reverence you on earth. Hail Mary . . .

7. Rejoice, O Mother, Daughter, and Spouse of God, because all the joys, graces, and favors that you enjoy in heaven will never undergo any diminution but will continue to rejoice your blessed heart for an endless eternity, Hail Mary . . . ; Glory be . . .

To Our Lady of Consolation

O Mary, most sweet, most amiable, and most glorious, your name cannot be uttered in the secret of the heart without inflaming it with your love; and those who love you cannot think of you without feeling animated to love you more and putting all their confidence in you.

Mary, my Mother, you see my trouble; look upon me with an eye of pity. You are the consolation of all who call upon you in times of affliction; be my consolation as well. Graciously hear the prayers of my poor heart; do not abandon me but support me in affliction and strengthen me in danger.

Mother of consolation, give peace to my soul; grant me all that you know I ask of you: obtain for me, from your divine Son, the pardon of all my sins, the grace to sin no more, the blessedness to imitate your virtues all the rest of my life, and finally a holy and a happy death. Mother Mary, I ask this as your child. I love you and I desire to make you loved by all hearts. Amen.

The Rosary

The Rosary of Our Lady is the spiritual sword wielded by Catholics all over the world. Carry a rosary in your pocket, and pray it often. The following meditations were composed by Paul Thigpen for his Manual for Spiritual Warfare. His meditations, rich in biblical imagery and a martial spirit, will help you contemplate the "stakes" of the battle we all must fight with our ultimate adversary, the Devil, for women are warriors too.

The Joyful Mysteries

THE ANNUNCIATION OF THE ANGEL GABRIEL TO OUR LADY

And the angel said to her, "Do not be afraid, Mary, for you have found grace with God. Behold, you

shall conceive in your womb and shall bring forth a Son; and
you shall call His name Jesus. He shall be great, and shall be
called the Son of the Most High; and the Lord God will give
Him the throne of David His father . . . and of His kingdom
there will be no end" (Lk 1:30–33).

The first Eve believed the lies of the Serpent,
and so began the battle with our ancient Enemy for
the eternal destiny of her children (see Gen 3:1–7).
But Our Blessed Lady, the new Eve, believed God's
word, announced by the angel Gabriel. By faith she
conceived the Son of God, who crushed the Serpent's head and won a kingdom that will never end.

Have I too placed my faith in that King? Have I
committed myself to do battle for His kingdom?

THE VISITATION OF OUR LADY TO ELIZABETH

And Mary said, "My soul magnifies the Lord, and
my spirit rejoices in God my Savior . . . because He
who is mighty has done great things for me, and holy is His
name. . . . He has shown might with His arm, He has scattered the proud in the conceit of their heart, He has put down
the mighty from their thrones, and exalted the lowly" (Lk
1:46–47, 49, 51–52).

God created the angelic hosts and gave them
heavenly thrones of power and authority to admin-
ister creation for Him. But the angel Lucifer and
his allies imagined in their wicked pride that they
could rebel against God and take His place (see
Is 14:12–15). When Our Lady met Elizabeth, she

praised God's saving power, who scattered the proud demons, cast them down to hell from their thrones, and raised up instead the redeemed of the lowly human race, so that we might reign with Him.

Have I joined our Blessed Mother in that song of praise? Do I share her confidence in God's triumph over evil?

THE NATIVITY OF OUR LORD

For this reason the Son of God appeared, that He might destroy the works of the Devil (1 Jn 3:8).

Heaven's strategy to overthrow Satan's kingdom was brilliant in its humility: The glorious Son of God came to earth quietly, not in a king's palace or a grand temple, not adorned in gold and purple, but born to an obscure peasant girl, wrapped in makeshift clothes, laid in a dusty manger. In his immense pride, the Devil was taken by surprise: He could not understand, he could not anticipate, that God would humble Himself this way for the sake of a weak and wayward human race (see 1 Cor 1:26).

Does my pride make me vulnerable to Satan's snares? Or do I imitate Our Lord's humility, so that I too can confound the Enemy?

THE PRESENTATION OF OUR LORD IN THE TEMPLE

And Simeon blessed them and said to Mary, His mother, "Behold, this Child is destined for the fall and for the rise of many in Israel, and for a sign that shall be contradicted. And your own soul a sword shall pierce, so that the thoughts of many hearts may be revealed" (Lk 2:34–35).

When Our Lady and St. Joseph presented Jesus in the temple, the aged Simeon warned them of the great spiritual conflict that had begun. In the fierce warfare between the Dawn from on High and the rulers of darkness (see Lk 1:78; Eph 6:12), many would rise and many would fall; and the mother of our Champion would herself bear unspeakable wounds in union with His agony on the field of battle.

When I am wounded in battle, do I join my suffering to that of our Blessed Mother and her Son? Do I recognize that only by God's grace can I be numbered among those who rise, rather than those who fall?

THE FINDING OF OUR LORD IN THE TEMPLE

And not finding Him, they returned to Jerusalem in search of Him. And it came to pass after three days they found Him in the temple, sitting in the midst of the teachers, listening to them and asking them questions. . . And He said to them, "How is it that you sought Me? Did you not know that I must be about My Father's business?" (Lk 2:45–46, 49).

Even at such a young age, Jesus knew who He was and what business He was about. He understood and embraced the mission His Father had given Him.

Am I aware of the battle that rages around me (see Eph 6:10–21)? How can I fight at Our Lord's side and share in His victory unless I too know my place in His army, recognize my mission, and follow His commands?

The Luminous Mysteries

THE BAPTISM IN THE JORDAN

And Jesus, full of the Holy Spirit, returned from the Jordan, and was led by the Spirit through the desert for forty days, being tempted by the devil (Lk 4:1–2).

At His baptism, Jesus was honored by the Father with words of affirmation from heaven, and the Holy Spirit filled Him with power. Yet even then, the Enemy was awaiting his chance to tempt the Savior, and he made his move soon afterward. Through prayer, fasting, and His knowledge of Scripture, Our Lord won the contest, and the Devil withdrew in defeat.

Do I ask the Holy Spirit's assistance in my own struggle against temptation? Have I taken up Christ's weapons of prayer, fasting, and Scripture?

THE MIRACLE AT CANA

And on the third day a marriage took place at Cana of Galilee, and the mother of Jesus was there. Now Jesus too was invited to the marriage, and also His disciples. . . . His mother said to the attendants, "Do whatever He tells you" (Jn 2:1–2, 5).

Turning water to wine at Cana was the first of Jesus' miracles. In the following days of His ministry, He undid the works of the Devil as He continued His miraculous deeds, healing the sick, raising the dead, casting out demons, and demonstrating in other ways His divine power over evil.

Am I willing to accept a share in Christ's saving power so I can help to set the captives free from bondage to the Enemy (see Lk 10:17–19)? In exercising that power, am I willing to follow Our Lady's instructions to do whatever Jesus tells me?

THE PROCLAMATION OF THE KINGDOM

Jesus came into Galilee, preaching the gospel of the kingdom of God and saying, "The time is fulfilled, and the kingdom of God is at hand. Repent and believe in the gospel" (Mk 1:14–15).

To deliver us from the dominion of darkness and transfer us into the kingdom of light (see Col 1:13), Jesus did more than work miracles; He preached the gospel as well. This gospel—this good news—was the announcement that through His life, passion, death, and resurrection, the incarnate Son of God had come to defeat the powers of evil, to vanquish sin and death. Then as now, such a proclamation demands a response of faith.

Do I firmly believe this good news? Am I a witness who declares it to others, so that more and more, the righteous reign of God is extended throughout the earth?

THE TRANSFIGURATION

*A*s He was still speaking, behold, a bright cloud overshadowed them, and behold, a voice out of the cloud said, "This is My beloved Son, in whom I am well pleased; hear Him." And on hearing it the disciples fell on their faces and were greatly afraid. And Jesus came near and touched them and said to them, "Arise, and do not be afraid" (Mt 17:5–7).

A divine intervention on the Mount of Transfiguration startled and terrified the three apostles who witnessed Christ's stunning radiance there. They were paralyzed by fright, so that Jesus had to touch them and tell them not to be afraid. His call to courage would soon prove all the more urgent: They descended from the glory on the mountain to confront a demon down in the valley, where their lack of faith hindered them.

Am I prepared to overcome my fear when the spiritual warfare between heaven and hell rages fiercely all around me, or am I tempted to flee in terror? Have I asked the Lord, as the Apostles did, to increase my faith (see Lk 17:5)?

THE INSTITUTION OF THE EUCHARIST

*F*or as often as you shall eat this bread and drink the cup, you proclaim the death of the Lord, until He comes (1 Cor 11:26).

When Our Lord instituted the Eucharist, He placed in the hands of His Church an incomparable weapon in her warfare with the Evil One. His death on Calvary was to be the supreme defeat and humiliation of the forces of darkness, so that ever after, demons would shrink from the emblem of the Cross. How much more, then, do they tremble even at the thought of the altar, in whose Holy Sacrifice that all-conquering death is both proclaimed and re-presented, until the Lord returns to earth in His final triumph over evil?

Am I partaking of the Eucharist worthily, faithfully, and frequently, so that the Enemy of my soul is firmly repulsed (see 1 Cor 11:27–32)? Do I avail myself of the powerful graces of the other sacraments as well?

The Sorrowful Mysteries

THE AGONY IN THE GARDEN

And there appeared to Him an angel from heaven to strengthen Him. And falling into an agony He prayed all the more earnestly. And His sweat became like drops of blood running down upon the ground. And rising from prayer He came to the disciples and found them sleeping for sorrow. And He said to them, "Why do you sleep? Rise and pray, so that you may not enter into temptation" (Lk 22:43–46).

In the hour of His greatest trial, Our Lord was no doubt tempted by the Devil to turn away from the cup of horror that He must drink. He prayed earnestly, and His Father answered those prayers through the ministry of an angel sent to strengthen Him. Meanwhile, the disciples had allowed their deep sorrow to numb them; having failed to pray that they would not enter into temptation, they would soon succumb to it, abandoning their Master to His murderers.

Do I seek the powerful assistance of the angels and saints when I must wage war against the Enemy's temptations and other assaults? Do I ever allow sorrow, fear, or doubt to paralyze me so that I falter in prayer?

THE SCOURGING AT THE PILLAR

B ut He was wounded for our transgressions, He was bruised for our iniquities; upon Him was the chastisement that made us whole, and with His stripes we are healed. . . . Therefore I will divide Him a portion with the great, and He shall divide the spoil with the strong, because He poured out His soul to death (Is 53:5, 12).

How sharp is the grief of realizing that Our Lord was scourged because of my sins! And yet how sweet is the consolation of knowing that by His stripes, my sins are forgiven, my soul is healed, and my spiritual Adversary is overthrown. The meek Lamb of God who poured out His soul to death has become the conquering Lion of Judah who divides the spoil with the strong (see Rv 5:5–10).

Am I faithful to seek God's mercy often through the Sacrament of Reconciliation (see Jas 5:16) so that, through Christ's stripes, I can be healed? Do I make a sincere confession and practice heartfelt penance to strengthen my will against the snares of the Tempter?

THE CROWNING WITH THORNS

A nd I saw heaven standing open; and behold, a white horse, and He who sat upon it is called Faithful and True, and with justice He judges and wages war. And His eyes are like a flame of fire, and on His head are many diadems. . . . He is clothed in a garment sprinkled with blood . . . And He has on His garment and on His thigh a name written, "King of kings and Lord of lords" (Rv 19:11–12, 16).

The crown of thorns placed in mockery upon Our Lord's head is now transformed: The Lamb who was slain comes as a conquering Warrior King, wearing glorious diadems on His head, with His robe dipped in the precious Blood whose irresistible power crushes the demon host. All authority in heaven and on earth is now His, and every knee must bow, every tongue confess that He is King of kings and Lord of lords (see Phil 2:10–11).

Do I find courage to persevere daily in the strength of this divine Warrior, my King? Do I hope in His promise that those who share His triumph will one day exchange their own thorny crowns for glorious crowns of righteousness (see 2 Tm 4:8)?

THE CARRYING OF THE CROSS

*B*ut as for me, God forbid that I should glory except in the cross of our Lord Jesus Christ, through whom the world is crucified to me, and I to the world (Gal 6:14).

The spiritual battle is waged not just against the Devil but also against "the passions of the flesh, which wage war against [the] soul" (1 Pt 2:11), and the false attractions of the world, which we must fight to overcome (see 1 Jn 5:4–5). To combat these enemies, Our Lord calls us to deny ourselves and take up our own cross—a share in His cross—in order to follow Him (see Mt 16:28). Through daily, sacrificial self-denial, the flesh and the world become dead to us, and we to them.

Do I make self-denying sacrifices, seeking the detachment that will allow me to triumph over the flesh and the world? Do I see my sufferings as splinters of Christ's cross, to be born with patience and hope?

THE CRUCIFIXION

*B*ecause children have blood and flesh in common, so He in the same way has shared in these, so that through death He might destroy him who had the empire of death, that is, the Devil; and might deliver them who, throughout their life, were kept in servitude by fear of death (Heb 2:14–15).

Fear of losing someone or something we love can enslave us, weakening our will to choose what is right. So fear of death is the greatest bondage of all, because death poses as the loss of all we hold dear. But on the Cross, God Himself has tasted death on our behalf, mastering it and overcoming the Enemy through whom death first entered the world. Death has lost its power over us, because we know that beyond death lies life everlasting for those who are in Christ.

Can I face the Devil without fear because I know that his weapon of death has lost its sting (see 1 Cor 15:55)? Do I firmly believe that all those who share in Christ's death will also share in His resurrection (see Rom 6:5)?

The Glorious Mysteries

THE RESURRECTION OF OUR LORD

Christ has risen from the dead, the first-fruits of those who have fallen asleep. . . . For as in Adam all die, so in Christ all will be made to live. But each in his own turn, Christ as first-fruits, then those who are Christ's, who have believed, at His coming. Then comes the end, when He delivers the kingdom to God the Father, when He does away with all sovereignty, authority, and power. For He must reign until "He has put all things under His feet" (1 Cor 15:20, 22–25).

If Christ had not been raised from the dead, our faith would be futile (see 1 Cor 15:17). The Devil, wielding death as his weapon, would have won the battle for our redemption, and all would be lost. But Christ has indeed been raised, and the head of the ancient Serpent was crushed by the stone that rolled away from the empty tomb. That morning saw the dawn of a new creation, in which every power opposed to God will at last be vanquished, and the One who triumphed over the grave will reign forever.

When the world all around me appears to be still in the grip of the Evil One, do I hold fast to the hope that his days are numbered? When the Devil reminds me of my past, do I remind him of his future?

THE ASCENSION OF OUR LORD

Thus it says, "Ascending on high, He led away captives; He gave gifts to men.". . . He who descended, He it is who ascended also above all the heavens, that He might fill all things (Eph 4:8, 10).

The ascension of Our Lord was the return of the King of Glory to His eternal throne. As heaven's gates were thrown open to receive Him, He brought in His train His vanquished demonic foes in chains. Like the victorious kings of old, Christ made a spectacle for all the subjects of His kingdom to watch, for through the Cross He had disarmed the demonic principalities and powers, and made a public example of them (see Col 2:15).

If Christ is now triumphantly seated at the Father's right hand in heaven, where He intercedes for us, am I confident of His powerful intercession for me? Am I certain that in Him, I am more than a conqueror, and nothing—not even demonic angels, principalities, and powers—can separate me from the love of God in Christ Jesus (see Rom 8:34, 37–39)?

THE DESCENT OF THE HOLY SPIRIT

And I send forth upon you the promise of My Father. But wait here in the city, until you are clothed with power from on high (Lk 24:49).

Who descended at Pentecost to clothe the disciples with power? It was the same Holy Spirit of God who had broken the Israelites' bondage and delivered them from death when He parted the Red Sea and overwhelmed Pharaoh's chariots; the Spirit who had come upon the warrior judges of old to defeat the enemies of God's people, and had come upon young David to vanquish Goliath; the Spirit by whose power Our Lady had conceived the Savior, and by whose power the Savior had been raised from the dead.

Do I try to fight this fierce spiritual war on my own? Or do I rely on the Holy Spirit's unlimited power to overcome my foes, because He who is in me is greater than he who is in the world (see 1 Jn 4:4)?

THE ASSUMPTION OF OUR LADY

*A*nd the dragon stood before the woman who was about to bring forth, so that when she had brought forth he might devour her son. And she brought forth a male child, who is to rule all nations with a rod of iron; and her child was caught up to God and to His throne. And the woman fled into the wilderness, where she has a place prepared by God. . . . And the dragon was angered at the woman, and went away to wage war with the rest of her offspring (Rv 12:4–6, 17).

In the Book of Revelation, the great panorama of our spiritual battlefield unfolds, displaying the age-old enmity between the Serpent and the Woman. Our Blessed Lady, clothed with the sun (see Rv 12:1), enters the fray by giving birth to the Warrior King. The Dragon, that ancient Serpent, seeks to swallow her Son in the tomb, but He breaks free from the bonds of death and ascends to His heavenly throne. His mother, too, escapes the Devil's grasp; her body defies death's corruption, and with her soul is assumed into heaven to join her Son.

If I remain in Christ, my mortal body will also put on immortality and be clothed with the radiance of heaven (see 1 Cor 15:53–55; Dan 12:2–3). But while the Dragon still makes war with me here on earth, am I making that body a weapon of righteousness?

Or am I yielding it to my spiritual enemies to use against me (see Rom 6:12–14)?

THE CROWNING OF OUR LADY AS QUEEN OF HEAVEN

He who overcomes, I will permit him to sit with Me upon My throne; as I also have overcome and have sat with My Father on His throne (Rv 3:21).

The King of the universe, having returned to His throne in heaven, welcomed Our Lady there as His Queen Mother. Full of grace, she had conquered the ancient Serpent, and so He fulfilled His promise to crown her with a share in His unfading glory (see 1 Pt 5:4), and to seat her at His side on His throne. Yet even though her place there is unrivaled, far above the angels and other saints, she waits to welcome all her children to their own abundant share in her Son's glory and authority.

Do I turn with trust to the Queen of Heaven to intercede for me and assist me, the Queen of the angels who continually come to my aid? Do I recognize that even now, because I am in Christ, I am seated with Him in heavenly places, far above all rule and authority, power and dominion (see Eph 1:16–22, 2:5–6)?

After the prayers of this final decade, conclude with these additional prayers:

Hail, Holy Queen . . .
St. Michael, the Archangel . . .

Angel of God, my guardian dear . . .

And this final acclamation:

Christ conquers! Christ reigns! Christ rules!

OTHER PRAYERS

Are not all angels spirits in the divine service, sent to serve for the sake of those who are to inherit salvation? Heb 1:14

Prayer to My Angel Guardian

O holy angel, to whose care God, in his mercy, has committed me, you who assists me in my needs, consoles me in my afflictions, supports me when disheartened, and who constantly obtains new favors for me—I return to you my sincere and humble thanks. I call upon you, my friend and guide, to continue your care for me, to defend me from my enemies and from my own poor inclinations, and to offer me the wisdom and humility to submit to the will of God. Amen.

Prayer to St. Joseph

O great saint, wise and faithful servant whom God has charged with the care of His family; you whom he has made guardian and protector of the life of Jesus, consoler and support of his Mother, and his faithful associate in the great design of our redemption; you who happily lived with Jesus and Mary, and passed away peacefully in their arms; chaste spouse of the Mother of God; model for pure, humble, and interior souls—be touched with the confidence we have in you, and graciously accept our testimonies of devotion. We thank God for the favors he has bestowed on you and we ask, through your intercession, that we may imitate your virtues. Pray for us, then, O glorious saint, and by the love you always had for Jesus and for Mary, and which Jesus and Mary had also for you, obtain for us the priceless gift of living and dying in their holy love. Amen.

Invocations to Saint Rita

St. Rita, Advocate of the Hopeless, pray for us.
St. Rita, Advocate of the Impossible, pray for us.
   Three Our Fathers,
   Three Hail Marys,
   Glory be to the Father . . .
Blessed be God, the Father of our Lord Jesus Christ, Father of Mercy and God of all Consolation, who, through the intercession of St. Rita, comforts us in all our tribulations. Amen.

Litany of Humility

O Jesus, meek and humble of heart, Hear me.

From the desire of being esteemed, Deliver me, O Jesus.

From the desire of being loved, Deliver me, O Jesus.

From the desire of being extolled, Deliver me, O Jesus.

From the desire of being honored, Deliver me, O Jesus.

From the desire of being praised, Deliver me, O Jesus.

From the desire of being preferred to others, Deliver me, O Jesus.

From the desire of being consulted, Deliver me, O Jesus.

From the desire of being approved, Deliver me, O Jesus.

From the fear of being humiliated, Deliver me, O Jesus.

From the fear of being despised, Deliver me, O Jesus.

From the fear of suffering rebukes, Deliver me, O Jesus.

From the fear of being calumniated, Deliver me, O Jesus.

From the fear of being forgotten, Deliver me, O
     Jesus.
From the fear of being ridiculed, Deliver me, O
     Jesus.
From the fear of being wronged, Deliver me, O
     Jesus.
From the fear of being suspected, Deliver me,
     O Jesus.

That others may be loved more than I, Jesus,
     grant me the grace to desire it.
That others may be esteemed more than I,
     Jesus, grant me the grace to desire it.
That, in the opinion of the world, others may
     increase, and I may decrease,
Jesus, grant me the grace to desire it.
That others may be chosen, and I set aside,
     Jesus, grant me the grace to desire it.
That others may be praised, and I go unnoticed,
     Jesus, grant me the grace to desire it.
That others may be preferred to me in
     everything, Jesus, grant me the grace to
     desire it.
That others may become holier than I, provided
     that I may become as holy as I should,
     Jesus, grant me the grace to desire it.

MERRY CARDINAL DEL VAL

*The faithful with deep spiritual affection are drawn to
commemorate the mysteries of divine pardon and to celebrate*

them devoutly. They clearly understand the supreme benefit, indeed the duty, that the People of God have to praise Divine Mercy with special prayers and, at the same time, they realize that by gratefully performing the works required and satisfying the necessary conditions, they can obtain spiritual benefits that derive from the Treasury of the Church. "The paschal mystery is the culmination of this revealing and effecting of mercy, which is able to justify man, to restore justice in the sense of that salvific order which God willed from the beginning in man, and through man, in the world" (Encyclical Letter, Dives in Misericordia).[73]

Divine Mercy Chaplet

The Divine Mercy chaplet is prayed on your Rosary beads. Begin with the Sign of the Cross.

Optional opening prayers:

You expired, Jesus, but the source of life gushed forth for souls, and the ocean of mercy opened up for the whole world. O Fount of Life, unfathomable Divine Mercy, envelop the whole world and empty Yourself out upon us.

---

73 Archbishop Luigi De Magistris, "Decree on Indulgences Attached to Devotions in Honour of Divine Mercy," accessed September 17, 2018, http://www.vatican.va/roman_curia/tribunals/apost_penit/documents/rc_trib_appen_doc_20020629_decree-ii_en.html.

O Blood and Water, which gushed forth from the Heart of Jesus as a fountain of Mercy for us, I trust in You! (Repeat 3 times)

Now begin:

Our Father, etc.
       Hail Mary, etc.
The Apostles' Creed (I believe in God, the Father Almighty, etc.)

On the large bead before each decade, pray:

Eternal Father, I offer you the Body and Blood, Soul and Divinity of Your Dearly Beloved Son, Our Lord, Jesus Christ, in atonement for our sins and those of the whole world.

One each small bead of the decade, pray:

For the sake of His sorrowful Passion, have mercy on us and on the whole world.
Pray five decades in total.

Concluding prayer:

Holy God, Holy Mighty One, Holy Immortal One, have mercy on us and on the whole world. (Repeat 3 times)

Optional closing prayer:

Eternal God, in whom mercy is endless and the treasury of compassion inexhaustible, look kindly upon us and increase Your mercy in us, that in difficult moments we might not despair nor become despondent, but with great confidence submit ourselves to Your holy will, which is Love and Mercy itself.

For a Friend in Tribulation

Grant, merciful Creator, the sweetness of your comforts to your troubled servant [name] and remove, according to Your accustomed mercy, the heavy burden of [his or her] calamities. I humbly ask that You grant him patience and perseverance in his sufferings and resignation to Your will. I ask this in Your loving son, Jesus's name. Amen.

Prayer of St. Teresa

My God! since You are charity itself, perfect this virtue in me, that its passion may consume all of self-love. May I hold You as my sole treasure and my one glory, far dearer than all creatures. Make me love myself in You, for You, and by You. Let me love my neighbor in the same way, for Your sake, bearing his burdens as I wish him to bear mine. Let me care for naught beside You, except insofar as it will lead me to You. May I rejoice in Your perfect love for me, and in the eternal love borne for You by the angels and saints in heaven, where the veil is lifted, and they see You face to face. Grant that I may rejoice because the just, who know You by faith in this life count You as their highest good, the center and the end of their affections. I long that sinners and the imperfect may do the same, and with the aid of Your grace I crave to help them.

ST. TERESA OF AVILA

HYMNS AND POEMS

POEMS

Divine Beauty

A poem by St. Teresa of Avila

hermosura que excedeis!

Beauty that doth far transcend
   All other beauty! Thou doest deign,
Without a wound, our hearts to pain —
Without a pang, our wills to bend
To hold all love for creatures vain.

O mystic love-knot that dost bind
Two beings of such diverse kind!
How canst Thou, then, e'er severed be?
For bound, such strength we gain from Thee,
We take for joys the griefs we find!

Things void of being linked, unite
With that great Beauty Infinite:
Thou fill'st my soul, which hungers still:

Thou lov'st where men can find but ill:
Our naught grows precious by Thy might!

"Soul, Thou Must Seek Thyself in Me, and Seek for Me in Thee."
A poem by St. Teresa of Avila

Alma, buscarte has en mi.

Such is the power of love, soul,
To paint thee in My heart,
No craftsman with such art,
Whate'er his skill might be, could there
Thine image thus impart!
'Twas love that gave thee life:
Then, Fairest, if thou be
Lost to thyself, thou'lt see
Thy portrait in My bosom stamped:
Soul, seek thyself in Me!

Wouldst find thy form within My heart
If there thou madest quest,
And with such life invest,
Thou wouldst rejoice to find thee thus
Engraven in My breast.
Or if, perchance, art ignorant
Where thou mayst light on Me,
Wander not wide and free,
Soul, if My presence wouldst attain,
Seek in thyself for Me!

Because in thee I find My house of rest,
My dwelling-place, My home,
Where at all hours I come
And knock at the closed portal of thy thoughts
When far abroad they roam.
No need is there to look for Me without,
Nor far in search to flee;
Promptly I come to thee;
If thou but call to Me it doth suffice—
Seek in thyself for Me!

HYMNS

Holy Virgin Mary

A hymn by St. Francis of Assisi

Holy Virgin Mary, there is none like you
among women born in the world.
Daughter and handmaid of the heavenly Father,
almighty King,
Mother of our most high Lord Jesus Christ,
Spouse of the Holy Spirit,
pray for us to your most holy Son, our Lord and
Master.
Hail holy Lady, most noble Queen,
Mother of God and Mary ever Virgin.

You were chosen by the heavenly Father,
who has been pleased to honor you

with the presence of his most holy Son
and the Divine Paraclete.
You were blessed with the fullness of grace and
    goodness.
Hail, Temple of God,
His dwelling place,
His masterpiece,
His handmaid.

Hail, Mother of God,
I venerate you for the holy virtues that,
through the grace and light of the Holy Spirit,
you bring into the hearts of your devoted ones
to change them from unfaithful Christians
to faithful children of God. Amen.

Bring Flowers of the Rarest
By Mary E. Walsh

Bring flowers of the rarest
bring blossoms the fairest,
from garden and woodland and hillside and dale;
our full hearts are swelling,
our glad voices telling
the praise of the loveliest flower of the vale!

Refrain:

O Mary! we crown thee with blossoms today,
Queen of the Angels, Queen of the May,

O Mary! we crown thee with blossoms today,
Queen of the Angels, Queen of the May.

Our voices ascending,
In harmony blending,
Oh! Thus may our hearts turn
Dear Mother, to thee;
Oh! Thus shall we prove thee
How truly we love thee,
How dark without Mary
Life's journey would be.

Refrain

O Virgin most tender,
Our homage we render,
Thy love and protection,
Sweet Mother, to win;
In danger defend us,
In sorrow befriend us,
And shield our hearts
From contagion and sin.

Refrain

Of Mothers the dearest,
Oh, wilt thou be nearest,
When life with temptation
Is darkly replete?
Forsake us, O never!

Our hearts be they ever
As Pure as the lilies
We lay at thy feet.

Refrain[74]

Splendor of the Father's Glory

Morning shines with Eastern light,
Earth is glad the day to see,
Flee ye phantoms of the night,
Thoughts and deeds of darkness flee.

So, when breaks our latest morn,
And we rise our Lord to meet,
Songs shall welcome in its dawn,
Shouts of joy its coming greet.

Glory to the Father be,
Equal glory to the Son,
With the Spirit, One and Three,
While eternal ages run. Amen.[75]

R. CAMPBELL

---

74 Sodality of the Blessed Virgin Mary, St. Basil's Hymnal (Toronto; Medina, NY: St. Michael's College; Jas. Brennan, 1897), 165.

75 Sidney S. Hurlbut, Treasury of Catholic Song: Comprising Some Two Hundred Hymns from Catholic Sources Old and New (New York: J. Fischer & Bro., 1915), 1, http://archive.org/details/treasuryofcatholoohurl.

My Song of To-Day
A hymn by St. Thérèse of Lisieux

Oh! how I love Thee, Jesus! my soul aspires
    to Thee
And yet for one day only my simple prayer I
    pray!
Come reign within my heart, smile tenderly on
    me,
To-day, dear Lord, to-day.

But if I dare take thought of what the morrow
    brings
That fills my fickle heart with dreary, dull
    dismay;
I crave, indeed, my God, trials and sufferings,
But only for to-day!

O sweetest Star of heaven! O Virgin, spotless,
    blest,
Shining with Jesus' light, guiding to Him my
    way!
O Mother! 'neath thy veil let my tired spirit rest,
For this brief passing day!

Soon shall I fly afar among the holy choirs,
Then shall be mine the joy that never knows
    decay;

And then my lips shall sing, to heaven's angelic
        lyres,
The eternal, glad To-day![76]

---

76 Sr. Thérèse, Carmelite of Lisieux, *Poems of Sr. Thérèse, Carmelite
    of Lisieux, Known as the "Little Flower of Jesus"*, trans. Susan L.
    Emery (Boston: Angel Guardian Press, 1907), 1.

A HEARTFELT THANK YOU TO ALL WOMEN FROM A SAINT

hank you, women who are mothers! You have sheltered human beings within yourselves in a unique experience of joy and travail. This experience makes you become God's own smile upon the newborn child, the one who guides your child's first steps, who helps it to grow, and who is the anchor as the child makes its way along the journey of life.

Thank you, women who are wives! You irrevocably join your future to that of your husbands, in a relationship of mutual giving, at the service of love and life.

Thank you, women who are daughters and women who are sisters! Into the heart of the family, and then of all society, you bring the richness of your sensitivity, your intuitiveness, your generosity and fidelity.

Thank you, women who work! You are present and active in every area of life-social, economic, cultural, artistic and political. In this way you make an indispensable contribution to the growth of a culture which unites reason and feeling, to a model of life ever open to the sense of "mystery", to the

establishment of economic and political structures
ever more worthy of humanity.

Thank you, consecrated women! Following the
example of the greatest of women, the Mother of
Jesus Christ, the Incarnate Word, you open yourselves with obedience and fidelity to the gift of
God's love. You help the Church and all mankind
to experience a "spousal" relationship to God, one
which magnificently expresses the fellowship which
God wishes to establish with his creatures.

Thank you, every woman, for the simple fact
of being a woman! Through the insight which is
so much a part of your womanhood you enrich the
world's understanding and help to make human
relations more honest and authentic.[77]

77 Pope St. John Paul II, Letter to Women, June 29, 1995,
   https://w2.vatican.va/content/john-paul-ii/en/letters/1995/
   documents/hf_jp-ii_let_29061995_women.html.